57 ORIGINAL AUDITIONS FOR ACTORS

A Workbook of Monologs for Professional & Non-professional Actors

by
EDDIE LAWRENCE

MERIWETHER PUBLISHING LTD.
Colorado Springs, Colorado

Meriwether Publishing Ltd., Publisher
P.O. Box 7710
Colorado Springs, CO 80933

Edited and coordinated by: Beth Archbold
Cover design: Michelle Z. Gallardo

© Copyright MCMLXXXIII Meriwether Publishing Ltd.
Printed in the United States of America
First Edition

Library of Congress Cataloging-in-Publication Data

Lawrence, Eddie, 1919-
    57 original auditions for actors.

    1. Monologues. 2. Acting. I. Title. II. Title:
Fifty-seven original auditions for actors.
PN2080.L34   1988   812'.54   83-62157
IBSN 0-916260-25-9

Preface

When I was a young actor making the rounds I was
constantly called on to audition. There were so many
actors out there looking for work that auditioning
became the only way for a producer or director to get
an idea of what an actor had to offer. I was stuck
because I always offered to do a monologue from "The
Last Mile." My trouble was that all the producers and
directors had heard this same monologue thousands of
times from tens of thousands of actors since the play was
first produced in the late twenties.

If there had been a book like this one, I would have been
very grateful and would probably have been a star of
the first magnitude twenty years sooner. As it is,
thirty-six years later, I'm still auditioning — and I'm not
kidding. Only now, I'm trying some of Eddie Lawrence's
auditions and I'm starting to make it.

Eddie has put together a great variety of pieces here that
could be very helpful to the young actor, especially.

Like it or not, we all have to audition some time or
another and in Fifty-Seven Original Auditions For Actors
you might just find one for you on a given occasion.

This is the true 57 Varieties — and that ain't ketchup!

Jason Robards

Table of Contents

1
Dropout

Disillusioned by life and his lackluster performance
in school there is nothing in sight that looks promising
to this teenager so he decides to drop out and go west.

My brother drives a truck he's doin' okay, yuh know?
My old man's in jail at least he's eatin' steady, yuh
know? I got three sisters and an uncle and an aunt
livin' with us all in the same crummy apartment.
It makes for a lotta' noise, yuh know? What good's
school unless yuh wanna be a lawyer or something an
that takes fifteen years right? Anyway I got no eyes for
that kinda 'tripe, yuh know? I got no eyes for nuthin'
except I do wanna get outta' here for keeps. Fast. I'm
just a burden around here yuh know? I know it, yuh
know? My brother's on my back my uncle's on my
back. Go to school inna day and work at night, go to
school at night an word inna daytime. Go to work get a
job yuh know? Me? I don't wanna go to school. I don't
wanna work. I don't wanna do nuthin' but travel maybe.
Yuh know? California. Up around San Francisco.
Maybe I'll get some work around there. I wouldn't
have this idea that I'm a burden, yuh know? Then
maybe I'll have some will tuh work, yuh know?
Here I'm at a friggin' impasse . . everyone barkin' at
me . . yuh know? Go to school . . go to work. Don't
go to school but get a job. Like what — a delivery boy?
I don't wanna be no soda jerk. Yuh know? So I think
I'll kiss my mother and get the frig outta' here right now.
I hope she don't wake up. I wouldn't know what to tell
her . . yuh know?

Spunky Romantic

This girl wants a taste of something else before settling
down. Telling her childhood sweetheart is difficult
but she gains confidence as she goes along.

Yes I want to be your wife Frank. And I love you. And
yes I want your children and a home and some sense of
direction in my life . . yes to all that. But please, Frank
darling . . not just yet. Let me cross the street . . by
myself . . and see what's on the other side. Afterwards
we'll be together for 110 years, I promise. Try not to
look so glum. I'm not going on a safari. I've got a
lovely place to stay and I'll write you every day and
if you'd only stop pulling that long face for a minute
I'll tell you all about it. Huh? Please . . Remember
Phyllis Horton? That's right the cheerleader . . well
she's got this spiffy apartment on Union Street in
San Francisco . . what do you mean you don't like it
already? Phyllis is willing to put me up till I find a
flat of my own. And she's got a friend named Alice
who works in this ad agency as an art director and she
thinks I can get a job there as a receptionist if I can
come up right away. You see the girl is pregnant . .
the receptionist, that is, and . . yes she's married —
what else? And Alice knows the boss real well . . in
fact he's crazy about her and it'll give me a chance
Frank to get a little experience on my own before
settling down so's I'll be able to handle everything
without surprises and regrets at what I didn't do or
couldn't do or haven't done but wanted to do . .
and please don't twist your lips again it raises havoc
with my nervous system. And don't torture yourself

1	*(contd)* about stupid things. There can be no other man.
2	How do I know? I just know! Well anyway I've made
3	up my mind — I'm going. Dear . . give me a little smile.
4	Please? Come on . . that's better. Bye. *(She walks off*
5	*slowly at first then with spirit)*
6	
7	
8	
9	
10	
11	
12	
13	
14	
15	
16	
17	
18	
19	
20	
21	
22	
23	
24	
25	
26	
27	
28	
29	
30	
31	
32	
33	
34	
35	

Taxi Driver

A cab driver has picked up an out-of-towner. A compulsive conversationalist he holds forth on his favorite topic, New York.

New York? I like it and I hate it. I love it and I despise it. New York. On one hand you can have a nice time in the Bronx Zoo — on the other hand you can get mugged in your bathroom. What can I tell you — I enjoy it and I'm disenchanted with it. Where else can you see Broadway Musicals featuring all the T.V. stars in the flesh and Japanese movies and museums with restaurants in them — and The Village is okay on weekends. The other side of the coin? Traffic tieups, mobbed buses, dinner costs an arm and a leg, can't take a stroll at night or find an apartment or a cop. You can have New York. You can have L.A. too. Unless you enjoy sitting on lawns with tears in your eyes from the smog. You need a car to buy a newspaper. You may not get mugged but Charles Manson's liable to drop in with a few cronies. Here you don't need a car but you could get shot in the subway. That's the way it goes. San Francisco? Essentially a small town with a wild trolley ride. Paris? If you don't speak French you're lucky if they let you in. London is a dream but then again I haven't been there. I can only speak from what I see in the movies and I'm sure that's slanted — right? Munich is nice probably if you're Hitler and Copenhagen you can have. Too far north. Freeze your pants off on Labor Day. Moscow you gotta stand in line an hour for a pretzel and Mexico's the birthplace of the tourista. So . . so it all comes down to what. New York! At least . . New York is New York!

Forgotten Movie Siren

A famous actress, down on her luck in later years, is
interviewed by a brash young casting director for a day's
shooting in a film. He's never heard of her and she is
set back bitterly.

What have I done? You're joking aren't you Mister
Webb? Didn't your daddy ever tell you about Priscilla
Fenton? What was he, a deep sea diver? Let's see . .
what have I done? I did Nora opposite Raymond
Massey in *Doll's House.* On Broadway — there wasn't
any off-Broadway in my day. Just On Broadway and
Out in Hollywood. Nothing in between except one big
county fair. What else have I done? Let's see . . I played
Ophelia to Barrymore's *Hamlet.* Which Barrymore?
Well it wasn't Ethel. Ethel? She was the sister of John
and Lionel. Sorry I couldn't bring any playbills but
they've become collectors items and they're in frames.
I did *Hell's Kitchen* opposite Jimmy Cagney when
he was very young and packed with explosive energy.
I worked with Clark Gable who was a pussy cat. Then
there was Bill Powell, a hell of an actor and a dream of
a man. Who's Bill Powell? William Powell. Never heard
of him either? Well, I'm in good company. *(Pause)*
Madames? Yes . . I've played madames . . of whorehouses
you mean . . yes . . I was in *Mademoiselle Fifi* opposite
George Arliss. George Arliss? Oh, he was a character
actor who did leads. Mademoiselle Fifi was a man.
Never heard of him or Fifi. No, I'm not angry . . it's a
compliment in a way. I've got the part. Good. By the
way, I don't appear in the nude or anything like that?
Oh . . well these days one never knows. One more thing . .
did you say Tuesday and Wednesday or Tuesday or
Wednesday? Just Wednesday. Thank you. Yes. I'm free.

Confession

This college boy has been keeping his ambition a secret
from his business oriented father. One night during a
man-to-man talk he lets it all hang out.

Dad I love you but I've made up my mind. I don't
want to be a lawyer. I don't think I can face sending a poor
guy to prison because he didn't pay his alimony or suing
someone for making a lot of noise at a party. And as
for the criminal cases that's life or death isn't it? I mean
I just know I am not equipped psychologically for that.
I take after mom. Live and let live — that's my
philosophy. And I don't know whether I can handle
the doctor bit either. I mean you've got to examine
people and tell them what they've got even though
they've got something horrible. You remember when
Charlie cut his hand that time? I was so put off by
the blood Dr. Binks treated me first. No . . I'm afraid
medicine's out. And I'm lousy in math. That takes
care of being an accountant or a scorekeeper . .
anything like that. And I'm a rotten dancer. And my
spelling's awful . . so I don't imagine I'd make a movie
critic though I know I wanted to be one in high school.
And I'm just not good enough at sports to turn pro
or even become a coach . . and I can't draw a straight
line . . But may I tell you something I do know? Music.
I feel it in my bones, dad. If you could stake me while
I form a rock group I think you'll be mighty happy
with your number one son. I just know I can make it
as a rock singer, dad. Sure I never took a lesson in my
life — but don't you see it doesn't make any difference!
Who cares?! Don't you get it dad? It's what you got in

1   *(contd)* here — and what comes out here! That's all
2   that matters! I'll let you in on another little secret.
3   Phil and Roger Burnside and little Betsy . . we've been
4   rehearsing in that big old barn at her cousin Terrence's
5   for five months and I think we're about ready to go!
6   Got a name and everything! We're calling ourselves
7   "Jack The Ripper!" Catchy isn't it? So dad all we
8   need now is about four or five thousand for costumes
9   and publicity and we're off to the races! We got an
10   agent and everything. Orville Crane . . you remember
11   Orville from the supermarket . . well he's a big agent
12   now! And he thinks we're going to be the next Rolling
13   Stones! Dad. Dad . . Hey ma you better come in here.
14   I think dad's sick or something. Looks like he passed out.
15
16
17
18
19
20
21
22
23
24
25
26
27
28
29
30
31
32
33
34
35

6
Waitress

A hard working girl who's used to saying what is on her mind. Clever and forthright she applies for a job in a chic restaurant.

Experience? Yess'r. Six months with the Reno Lounge . . that's downtown. That was my first job here in L.A. . Then a year at Angelo's and three months with the Macho Bar and Grill on The Strip. That was my last job. Yess'r — I quit. I wasn't too crazy about the hours. We went till four a.m. I got to look like Dracula's daughter. Well, I like to get home before midnight . . it's a quirk of mine. What, sir? Oh, no, I liked Angelo's. Only I got very heavy from all that Italian food and I figured it was time for a change anyway. Independent? I guess so. As a matter of fact I do speak a little French. Je suis tres heureuse a vous voir. More? Deux bifteks aux champignons . . a point. Merci . . merci beaucoup . . and when I get a real nice tip, merci millefois. That's about it except for Il fait beau n'est-ce pas? I once worked in a French takeout in Greenwich Village. Well the boss kinda liked me and he began baking tarts with my name on them. His wife got jealous and started to have me trailed. It's all so silly in retrospect. So I came out here to L.A. and took that job with the Reno Lounge. It was several steps down. Skid Row I called it. How late does Le Petite Maison stay open? Very civilized. Yes I know it's a class restaurant . . I've seen your ads. It certainly would be a welcome change but in all honesty after the Macho Bar and Grill MacDonald's would seem like the Bel Air. No I'm not married. And I promise I won't do anything to bring

1	*(contd)* disgrace upon Le Petite Maison . . if, that is, I
2	ever get to be part of your operation. I'm hired?
3	Thank you so much . . I know you'll be pleased with
4	my work. I'm very efficient. Oh, one thing — it's
5	"La" Petite Maison . . not "Le." Or do you do
6	that to attract attention?
7	
8	
9	
10	
11	
12	
13	
14	
15	
16	
17	
18	
19	
20	
21	
22	
23	
24	
25	
26	
27	
28	
29	
30	
31	
32	
33	
34	
35	

Wary Politico

*A smooth-talking, long-winded congressman examines
all sides of a shady proposition put forth by some
questionable types. He is intrigued but cautious.*

Now I know what you'd like me to do gentlemen . .
and I know lots of people in this town have done it —
but would I be acting in the best interests of my
constituents? In other words *(Clears throat)* is there
any possibility that through some fluke or unforseen
interpretation of the constitution I could be censured
or worse still — impeached? I'd hate to be impeached
you understand. It would not only be embarrassing it
might seriously impair my chances of being assigned a
post in the future such as commissioner of baseball
which I've had my eye on for several years. Yes I know
everybody does it and they're still around . . but these
are sensitive times. The opposition is champing at
the bit for the opportunity to nail some poor patsy
involved in something as controversial as inner city
oil drilling. *(Clears throat)* On the other hand, all I'd
actually be doing is authorizing the expenditure of a
million dollars for a project I have in essence supported
ever since I can remember. And if in appreciation of my
efforts in this matter you'd want to see that some . .
(Clears throat) . . spiritual remuneration . . came my
way . . well, I wouldn't be able to do much about that
would I? After all your generous reaction would not
be in return for my assistance . . it would have come
about because of my tenacious stand in the interest of
the public good during this shameless time of insidious
waffling and blatant opportunism. One is a quid pro quo

10

1   *(contd)* deal while the other is the normal response of
2   confreres sharing a sacred bond. *(Clears throat)* Well
3   now that we've clarified the issues here gentlemen ..
4   I've made up my mind. I cannot go through with it. I am
5   just frightened to death of the whole business. One
6   more thing .. no one in this room tape recorded me
7   did they? Cause I warn you — I'll plead entrapment!
8
9
10
11
12
13
14
15
16
17
18
19
20
21
22
23
24
25
26
27
28
29
30
31
32
33
34
35

Badgered Single

A lonely, but spirited girl at a party is the target of a
persistent fellow who's a bit tipsy. At first she is
annoyed but he begins to grow on her.

Now look honey . . there's no use knocking yourself
out I don't think you're my type. So please . . lay off . .
huh? Look there's a cute little chick at the punchbowl.
Why don't you give her a try? You like me? Well,
either you've got a lot of stamina or you're just stupid.
You agree? Okay let me try and state my case a little
more forcefully. I don't care for your looks, the way
you dress, your haircut . . I'm not particularly crazy
about your buck teeth and everything else about you
depresses me. Now beat it. *(Pause)* You can take it?
Look mister why do you persist? I'm simply not
interested in you. I know you like me . . you told me
that . . but you bore me. You remind me of an uncle
of mine who bores me. I don't like him and I don't
like you. Now blow. You're still mad about me?
What are you — a masochist or something? No,
I got nothing against masochists. I never met one until
now. Look at the sweet little number that just came
in with the cloth coat. She's better looking than I am
and I'll bet she's a terrific dancer. Go make eyes at her.
I remind you of your ex-wife? Well why not go back to
her? She's not your type? *(Laughs)* One thing mister
you do have an offbeat sense of humor. I see a girl over
there laughing . . let me introduce you. God you're
stubborn. You're rather droll actually. What are you
nodding and smiling at? You know something . . you're
beginning to grow on me. Gradually. Little by little . .

1 *(contd)* I'm getting used to you. *(Pause)* Would you
2 mind escorting me over to the punchbowl Mister
3 Whateveryournameis. I think I feel like partaking.
4
5
6
7
8
9
10
11
12
13
14
15
16
17
18
19
20
21
22
23
24
25
26
27
28
29
30
31
32
33
34
35

Visitor From London

This Britisher sings the Big Apple's praises to a friend
but gets carried away by thoughts of his native London
in the process. He has no outward bitterness but rather
a deep rooted conditioning that can't stay put.

Wonderful city your New York. Reminds me a bit of
London really. Fifth Avenue is rather like our Regent
Street you know. And down around Wall Street there
are certain similarities too. Then again there's nothing
here quite like Fleet or Old Bond, eh? They're typically
British. And Russell Square up in Bloomsbury . . that's
London for you. Of course there's the East End
something like your lower East Side I daresay . . but
essentially quite different. Still . . *(Pause)* Take our Big
Ben for instance. Nothing to touch it here. Actually,
you could set your watch by it day or night. No one
seems to care about the time in New York. That clock's
two and a half hours slow you see. This simply does
not happen in London. Is it the expense or just
carelessness? Still the two cities have a lot in common . .
except possibly for the parks. St. James and Hyde . .
not at all like your Central you know . . that is to say
they are actually cared for. Not that your Central isn't
looked after . . but you do get my drift . . St. James is
treated as though it were a handsome woman while
Central Park somehow brings to mind a flamboyant
character of some sort. Not that I mind it really . . it
gives the city a kind of Runyonesque texture if you
follow me. Naturally your theaters are sublime.
Then again in London during intermission there's
tea you know . . brought right to your place while you

1	*(contd)* wait for the second act to start. I tell you
2	there's no comparison so far as relaxation goes.
3	Take the subways. One may smoke in ours or even have
4	his dog along provided it's muzzled properly . . it's all
5	so much more civilized if you get my meaning. Less
6	of a chore. But please don't misunderstand me . . I
7	just love the Big Apple. Reminds me so much of
8	London. Ah here's a taxi now . . and speaking of
9	taxis . . .
10	
11	
12	
13	
14	
15	
16	
17	
18	
19	
20	
21	
22	
23	
24	
25	
26	
27	
28	
29	
30	
31	
32	
33	
34	
35	

Football Freak

She's in love with a football hero and doesn't care who
knows it. Her mother is a patient audience.

You never saw anything like him mom! The way he
took that ball on an interception and ran it back a
hundred and seven yards for a touchdown with the
crowd just screaming their heads off. He was like a . .
like a . .Greek God! I wish daddy could have been there.
It'd take some of the wind out of his sails I'll bet.
Always talking Peter down . . jabbering on about the
good old days when football was football and how
Peter wouldn't even make the scrub team in his day.
You were there mom. Was pop that good? You don't
know? What position did he play anyway . . every time
we talk it was somewhere else. You didn't notice? Boy,
he must have been a standout! It's still ringing in my
ears . . ten thousand people yelling as one — "All the
way Pete — all the way!" When I think I used to frown
on football and jocks . . all because of daddy. He made me
think athletes are egomaniacs and that all they want is
to be T.V. sportscasters. Well not Peter. Peter wants
to be either a lawyer or a movie star. You know what
he told me? I was his inspiration. He likes me a great
deal, mom . . and I wouldn't be surprised if one day
he asks me to marry him. I get that feeling from the
way he lowers his eyes everytime I say something
about how grand it would be to spend the rest of
your life with someone who gets you so excited.
Imagine mom . . Peter wins a scholarship to Ohio State
and becomes All-American and we get married and he
ends up with the Green Bay Packers. Gosh that

1	*(contd)* **sounds neat.** *(Holds her nose)* **Number forty-two-**
2	**Peter Stanley!** Now playing quarterback for Green
3	Bay! Honestly, I like pop but sometimes I could sock
4	him over the head with that motheaten pair of shoulder
5	pads he's got hanging up in his den! Good night mom.
6	
7	
8	
9	
10	
11	
12	
13	
14	
15	
16	
17	
18	
19	
20	
21	
22	
23	
24	
25	
26	
27	
28	
29	
30	
31	
32	
33	
34	
35	

Music Lover

A devotee of serious music, Grandpa now lives with
son's family who couldn't care less about his interests.
Stripped of his passion he complains to the greats. A
bitter man he nevertheless hasn't lost his sense of humor.

Hey -- Mozart! It's the end of an era! WQXR dropped
Symphony Hall! We're being overruled by a massive
silent majority of simple simons. You listening
Humperdinck? It's a conspiracy! The only time I
get to hear Vivaldi is when I sneak out to a double
feature and they use him as background to a horse race!
And the director is hailed as a genius! Tell me something —
Mahler! Why isn't my golden age card good for concerts?
Don't just lay there Stravinsky — do something about it!
Contact Leonard Bernstein by ESP! My grandson tells me
Tschaikowsky's heavy stuff. *(Chuckles) (Sings)* Full
moon and empty arms . . You hear Bela Bartok? You
mention Schoenberg around here, they think you're
talking about a vegetarian restaurant on the West
Side. Rod McKuen equals Brahms. Ask anyone. And
that theme from Elvira Madigan? Groovey! Chopin?
Easy . . *(Sings)* I'm always chasing rainbows . . you win
64 dollars. Planet of The Apes is a hit Sibelius! The
title is significant. Comedy sketches on T.V. about how
Franz Shubert couldn't finish a symphony hahahaha . . and
how he died at 32 and left his genius behind forever. Boy
is that funny. Hate to bother you Ludwig but they're using
(Sings) dum-dum-dum-dum for a commercial! Mark my
words if there's another war Radio Free Asia will sign
on with "I Ain't Nuthin' but A Hound Dog!" Listen
Johann Sebastian . . I heard some of your stuff the

1 *(contd)* other day . . emanating from the den. When
2 I looked in I saw two idiots on T.V. chasing each
3 other naked in the woods to a pascicaglia. The kids
4 were all excited. A breakthrough — they called it.
5 I said Bach on T.V.? No — they said . . nudity on
6 T.V. A significant happening grandpa. A landmark
7 in fact! I couldn't answer because today there is no
8 answer. *(Pause)* Scarlatti! You're better off dead!
9
10
11
12
13
14
15
16
17
18
19
20
21
22
23
24
25
26
27
28
29
30
31
32
33
34
35

Scars of War

1
2
3
4 *This disenchanted Neopolitan beauty meets her former*
5 *fiance, a repatriated POW, whom she still loves, and tells*
6 *him her tortured story.*
7
8
9 It was just after you were reported missing in action. The
10 Germans were everywhere and I was starving . . literally . .
11 eating grass, Paulo. Hiding out in a cave. Have you ever
12 spent a night in a cave? Well I was living there . . see?
13 So I . . I married this person whom you knew very well . .
14 this friend of my father's . . this collaborator if you like . .
15 just so I could eat regularly — you understand? And
16 live in a decent place. And he did care for me I guess
17 in his peculiar way . . and was even kind to me . . until
18 I started to resist his advances. It got so . . I couldn't
19 stand looking at him. His voice began to grate . . his
20 smell . . his touch disgusted me. And more important
21 I was disgusted with myself. He became crazy and kept
22 threatening to send me back to my cave. When I said
23 he could have his fun elsewhere that I wouldn't mind
24 he beat me black and blue. I told him I suddenly
25 realized I wasn't the woman for him after all . . that
26 the war did strange things to people. I didn't have the
27 courage to tell him the truth . . that I despised him but
28 I despised living like an animal even more, so I took the first
29 man with money I could think of. Then when we
30 found out you were being repatriated to work for The
31 Allies he said he was going to shoot us both. I told him
32 I was going to testify against him as a collaborator. That
33 night when I was asleep he got out his revolver and
34 aimed it at my head. He began to laugh hysterically
35 and suddenly he turned the gun upon himself.

1   *(contd)* I would never have testified against him anyway
2   because you see I was guilty as he was . . maybe
3   guiltier. That's my story Paulo. The rest is up to
4   you.
5
6
7
8
9
10
11
12
13
14
15
16
17
18
19
20
21
22
23
24
25
26
27
28
29
30
31
32
33
34
35

Engaging Barber

This gregarious fellow expertly wielding his scissors is
a bit of a philosopher as well as an authority on haircuts
and popular music. He is more or less in a position of
power, isn't he?

How do you want it — short — long? Medium. Where
do you want the part — on the side? In the middle? It's
only my opinion, of course, but I think it would look
better on the side. For your face. Of course, if you
want it in the middle, that's your business. *(Works the*
scissors) Middle parts went out of style years ago. Don
Ameche was the first guy to make the middle part popular,
though his was a titch to the right. Musta been 35, 40
years ago. Then came Ed Sullivan . . or did he part his
hair three-quarters? I don't remember . . *(Scissors)* But I
do remember they were both of the old school . . both
Don and Ed. *(Sings away)* Tomorrow . . Tomorrow . .
I'll love you tomorrow . . it's only a day awayyy . . You
say you want it medium? That's what I thought you said.
Just checking. *(Sings)* Tomorrow . . Tomorrow . . I'll love
you tomorr . . You don't mind me singin', do you? You
do. Well, maybe I got the wrong song for you. You
looked like a Tomorrow man. How about "Stardust"?
You hate "Stardust"? *(Sings)* Sometimes I wonder how
to spend those lonely hours . . How can you hate
"Stardust"? It's harmless. *(Scissors)* You like rock?
Punk? Just a thought. *(Scissors)* You don't like
classical? That's good, because I'm not too knowledgeable
on classical. Even though I craved an education, I
couldn't get one. My kids, thank the Lord, won't
have to worry about that. They got a father who

1   *(contd)* works with them in mind. About the only

2   thing I know in classical is *(Beethoven's Fifth Chords)*

3   Dum-Dom-Dom-Dom. Bum-Bom-Bom-Bom. Tricky

4   isn't it? Welp . . there you are sir. One medium

5   haircut with a part in the middle. OK? Oh, you really

6   don't have to tip sir. I own the place. But thanks

7   anyway. And call again. Next! How do you like it —

8   long — short? Nothing off the top. With your face I

9   don't know. But you're the doctor. It's just an

10   expression. *(Scissors) (Sings)* Tomorrow . . Tomorrow . .

11   I'll love ya tomorrow . . Like "you're the boss" . . *(Sings)*

12   It's only a dayy awayyy . . .

13

14

15

16

17

18

19

20

21

22

23

24

25

26

27

28

29

30

31

32

33

34

35

14

Bombshell

*This French bombshell is actually Hungarian. Under the
impression her current flame was grooming her to take
Bo Derek's place, she has discovered otherwise. Despite
her jazzy appearance she has something.*

No cheri — no. No hanky-panky tonight. Mellita is
very unhappy. When I have come to zis country you
say I am to act in movie wiz Robaire Redford —
N'est-ce pas? Let me finish. So I am very happy,
naturellement. I think I have chance to show everybody
Mellita is not only sex symbol, but also Mellita can
make audience cry. Now I find out I am to play in
film wiz Robaire Wilcox who I never hear about before
and who none of my brozzers or my mozzer have never
hear about before, and zey go to movies of all nations.
And not only I am to play wiz zis Robaire Wilcox who
nobody has ever hear about before, but aussi, I must come
out in night club in a bikini of feathers sitting on a donkey
and sing song called "I like papaya." I do not mind ze
song . . as a matter of fact I like papaya, cheri, but you
make me understand I am to act in dramatic feature
feelm about doctors and nurses wiz Robaire Redford, not
Robaire Wilcox, who I find out one hour ago is Olympic
sweemer who come out feefth in ze butterfly. So is a
whole new ballgame, cheri . . right? Let me finish. I have
not fly six thousand miles to be in X-rated peecture sitting
on donkey wiz feathers and singing song about papaya and
getting kidnapped by a gorilla and taken to Rio. I come
to appear in A-Peecture weeth Robaire Redford or Burt
Reynolds and make audience cry when I die in the end.
So what I have to say, cheri, is . . au revoir, monsieur.
Also, shave your beard off . . it looks silly. I am finish now.

15

Loser

A desperate plea from a perennial hanger-on who is not too keen on going it alone at this stage of his life.

It's just a matter of time. Then I'll buy you things, Rhoda. I'll buy you things. Sure it's been a while but that's just it — I'm due! I feel it in my bones. And you're going to be part of it. That's for being a real sticker all these years. I'm a sticker. That's why I'm gonna make it. There comes a time in this business when a guy clicks. Just like that. *(Snaps his fingers)* Even guys who are just survivors. They click. Just like that. *(Snaps)* I'm more than a survivor. I'm an active participant. Sure . . No need to panic. Look at Jerry Cranepool pluggin' that little digital computer that figures out the horses . . for fifteen years he's been going door to door until he meets this chap at a party and whap! Two hundred G's. If I were him I wouldn't have sold all the rights outright like that but there y'are — two hundred big ones. Boy, the things I could buy for you with that kind of scratch. It'll come. It'll come. I can taste it. Who knows — a few months from now I could be a millionaire. Because I never give up, Rhoda. I never give up the proverbial ship. You remember at first you didn't want to see me again but I persisted till I won you over — right Rhoda? And you know what I'm gonna do with all that dough — I'm gonna share it with you . . right down the middle . . because you're a sticker like me. True blue. So have a little patience with your friend Harvey and you won't regret it. Of course I'm not into computers and all that jazz but I've got this script here. Remember that one that

1	*(contd)* the kid in the parking lot wanted me to read?
2	Well it's a musical . . for off-Broadway. Sort of a
3	"Guys And Dolls" set in the year 2000. It'll run
4	forever and then there's secondary rights . . movies . .
5	All I need is a couple of grand for front money then
6	watch me roll. Rhoda . . Rhoda! I need you Rhoda!
7	Please don't leave me! Not now! Ahhh . . they're
8	all alike. No patience.
9	
10	
11	
12	
13	
14	
15	
16	
17	
18	
19	
20	
21	
22	
23	
24	
25	
26	
27	
28	
29	
30	
31	
32	
33	
34	
35	

Bored Wife

Suddenly everything catches up with this suburban
wife at once. She can't hold back any longer.

Don't you see dear? I'm bored. I'm bored with this
house, the view out the window, the way you dress,
and the way you say okey-dokey! It's driving me up
a wall! I can't stand our neighbors. The kids are driving
me crazy! I even hate the mailman! So please, I've got
to get away. Alone. I don't know . . Bermuda . . Paris . .
even Syracuse. Someplace where I can gather up the
pieces and think things over. I'm not getting any
younger you know . . or saner hanging around here.
Don't sit there chuckling! That chuckle will be my
undoing someday! What are you trying to hide? Afraid
to laugh out loud or you might break down and cry? Go
ahead — it'll do you some good! Scream! Yell! Get
hysterical — but please don't chuckle! I can't deal
with it. Heh-heh . . heh-heh . . holy cow! Everything's
going to be all right?! Everything's going to be all right?!
What are you — nuts? I'm coming apart at the seams here!
Everything's gonna be all right. You sound like somebody's
guru! Everything's gonna be all right. That's what they
said about Hitler! Look — I've made up my mind. I'm
packing my bags, booking a limo, and going straight to the
airport. Then I'm taking a plane to anywhere. When I get
to where I'm going I'll drop you a card. Don't try and
stop me because either I do that immediately or you'll
have to call in the mental health squad. No — I do not
want to see a marriage counselor! He's liable to tell us
everything's gonna be all right! Well it isn't Paul. It isn't!

Young Father

This man has been married a year. Since then he has
spent more time than usual in his favorite bar. He
pours his miserable heart out to his favorite bartender
after three doubles.

I don't know what to do anymore Gus. I don't love her.
I never did. All I wanted was to romance her a little.
Which I did. That night I met her at this very bar. You were
here Gus. Then, you want to know the actual facts Gus,
I didn't have the heart to tell her goodbye. Those are the
actual facts. I couldn't muster enough courage to call it
off. Those are the facts ma'am. I don't know. I'm
just a jerk with a heart of gold. At least I had a heart
of gold. Once. Now I'm a cynic. I've developed into
a real wiseguy. It's a defense. You understand? I'm
trapped into a life I despise and the only thing I can do
about it is crack bad jokes and booze. And now — with
this kid coming! How did I get into this predicament?
I don't love her Gus! And I've got to love the woman
I call my wife! I want someone to make me happy
when I get home from work! Where is she Gus? Who
is she? Aww, it doesn't make any difference anyway.
If I found her I wouldn't have the nerve to make the
break. Not with the kid coming. And what's worse is
she doesn't even know I don't love her. Boyyy wouldn't
it be great Gus . . if she didn't love me. That'd be
sensational. Then we could make some arrangement
after the kid's born. You think I'm a weakling? Tell
me Gus . . I've been coming in here for five years now
you can tell me if I'm a weakling or not. What would
you do in my place Gus? Relax? What kind of an

28

1   *(contd)* answer is that — relax? Give me another double
2   Gus. And leave it on the bar. I've got to make a
3   phone call. So she don't think I got caught in a train
4   wreck. Relax. No tip Gus. No tip tonight. I mean that
5   Gus.
6
7
8
9
10
11
12
13
14
15
16
17
18
19
20
21
22
23
24
25
26
27
28
29
30
31
32
33
34
35

Valedictorian

*A high school graduate falters in her valedictorian
address and has trouble with the prepared text, but
she manages to ad lib desperately . . and finish to a
somewhat bewildered reception.*

My dear faculty . . fellow students . . and honored guests
of Harrison High. It is indeed with . . *(Clears throat)*
actually with great sorrow, deep humiliation . . and an
actual lump in my throat . . that I bid a . . f-fond
f-farewell to Harrison High. *(Clears throat)* And it is
indeed . . with f-fond affection and . . and affectionate
f-fondness that we all look ahead to the past four years . .
four wonderful years . . and even with greater f-fondness
and f-affection that we gaze back on the next four —
or for that matter five . . or eight or even twelve
perhaps . . with pride . . and . . prejudice. *(Clears throat)*
For we at Harrison High will never forget the invaluable
teachings we were . . er . . taught — by our teachers —
in other words . . the faculty. How can we help but
remember dear Miss . . Miss Cranston, Mrs. Hartmann
er Hartley! And then there's Miss Cummings . . Mr.
Wrath . . er Roth! Mr. Cardiff and Miss . . pardon me
Mrs. Cardiff and Miss . . Miss . . oh how we miss
them all! Already! For they have given us . . they have
handed us the torch while it was still afire. And now it is
up to us . . to . . take this torch by the flame . . hand . .
handle! And not get burned . . scorched . . by it. And
now for our parents. They too have played their part
in the last four years . . by supporting us and giving us
room and board and in some cases allowances. They
have seen us through a crucial time . . to say nothing

1 *(contd)* of the four or six and in some cases ten or
2 twelve years to come. Though they may not know
3 it. And now . . to close . . I wish to lead you all in
4 our school cheer. *(Spells it out)* H-A-R-R-I-S-O-N . . .
5 Harrison! Yeahhh . . team! Thank you. *(Bursts*
6 *into tears)* That settles it — I'm never going to run
7 for the Senate! I just know it! *(Storms off)*
8
9
10
11
12
13
14
15
16
17
18
19
20
21
22
23
24
25
26
27
28
29
30
31
32
33
34
35

Small Town Editor

*This old timer despite his crusty tone is flattered that
a talented young writer should want to work on his little
newspaper. Deep down he wishes he had more ambition
when he was young.*

Son, I know you're from Chicago and they do things
big up that way. Lots of foreign news and sexy headlines.
Well, this here newspaper's interested more in the plain,
everyday folks of Woodhurst, birthplace of General
Meade. What they say . . who they marry . . who died
yesterday and if any of our lads is drafted. We're not
concerned if any movie star's kid calls her mother names.
Now if all this seems a little dull to you let me know and
we'll call it off and no hard feelings. Coffee? Sure, we're
interested in politics. We print all the president's speeches
as is and on Friday's we run a Europe page tellin' about
what's happenin' in Paris, London and Tokyo and whether
it's good for us. Alongside it we feature an in-depth
profile of a great American city . . sort of to balance
things off. My idea and I think it's a good one. We
need more imaginative concepts like that around here
son and frankly that's why I sent for you. I read some of
your college articles and they remind me of my stuff
at your age. I had all kinds of plans then. Even went
to New York. Anyway I wanted to speak to you face-
to-face. I know the salary isn't much but we'll keep you
busy and you might get some experience that you'll be
able to fall back on when you land that job with
Newsweek. Well, what do you say? You'll give it
your best shot? What's a shot? Okay . . good that's
all I can ask for. Now son your first assignment could

1   *(contd)* be kinda' exciting if you tackle it in the right
2   frame of mind. I want you to cover the annual cheddah
3   cheese eating contest at the Woodhurst Armory which
4   starts in exactly thirty-eight minutes. The winner gets
5   seventy-five dollars in saving bonds and a head of
6   General Meade carved in cheddah cheese. Anyone can
7   enter. Fine idea. Never thought of that. Sure you
8   can enter. Get the real inside story. Go to it boy!
9   See you later! *(Pause)* I guess the poor kid's hungry.
10
11
12
13
14
15
16
17
18
19
20
21
22
23
24
25
26
27
28
29
30
31
32
33
34
35

Delinquent

This poor soul is arrested for the third time in her young life.
She pleads with the judge to give her a chance to make
something of her life before it's too late. We feel she
means it.

Look your honor wherever you send me if it's around
this area again I'm gonna meet the same crowd with the
same ideas that got me in trouble in the first place and I'll
probably be back here before you know it. I'm tired of
hangin' out with losers who don't know nuthin' but
heists and how to forge credit cards and even more
terrible things, yuh know? I wanna see new faces your
honor. I wanna learn some kind of trade. I've had it
with playin' lookout for a bunch of crumbs who
think they got the system beat. Yeah . . this is the third
time I been here I know that. Three time loser . . but I
got this gut feelin' I could make it my last. Only . . if
I go back to the same bin with that ole gang o' mine I
just know it's gonna be too late your honor. As soon
as some big floosie with pimples comes over and tells
me she heard good things about me from so and so and
can't we rap I know what's gonna happen because
frankly I can't take it being a loner. I don't have that
kind of strength. I gotta belong, your honor . . yuh
know? Give me a break. Send me upstate to a work
camp or a correction ranch if there is some such place . .
and let me belong to it. And be around people who
want to better themselves. Believe it or not, your
honor, I get along good with strangers. I used to be an
usher. So at least let me have the opportunity to
show what I can do with myself . . if that's at all

1   *(contd)* possible. A change of climate? Somethin'?
2   I got nobody tuh keep me here . . no family tuh speak
3   of. Is that askin' too much your honor? Otherwise . .
4   I got a feelin' . . I may go right down the tube . .
5   yuh know? *(Pause)* Thank you your honor . . for
6   listening anyway.
7
8
9
10
11
12
13
14
15
16
17
18
19
20
21
22
23
24
25
26
27
28
29
30
31
32
33
34
35

Sarge

This gruff army veteran, conscious of some college men
in the ranks, tells a batch of recruits that they're in the
army now.

All right men, fall in. Alphabetically. Okay . . never
mind . . just line up. Anyway. Aatt's it. Now I
don't have to tell you men, the army is different from
home life. Your mother ain't here. Your father ain't
here. And your sister ain't here. But your big brother's
here. That's me. And I'm around all the time watchin'
you. So watch it. Now I don't mind in the beginin' if
you goof. We all goof. We're only human. *(Pause)*
Who said that? Wise guy inna crowd huh? Commentator.
Well we're gonna weed out all the commentators and
wits and wise guys an ship 'em to Tibbet. You know
where Tibbet is? Way wayyy up inna mountains. Men
have been known to freeze their ears off on a balmy
summer's eve. Those men were mainly wise guys.
There ain't no room in the army for wise guys an witty
commentators. There's only room in the army for
people willin' to loin. And there's plenny to loin in the
army. You loin to march. You loin how to fight. You
loin how to take orders . . an if you don't, you loin
how to clean latrines. That may come in handy later in
life especially if you're a wise guy. Now, when I say
tetch-hut! whatever you're doin' wherever you are
you snap to. I'm gonna pull that on yuhs today so
keep your thinkin' caps on I'm just warnin' yuhs. Now
as far as gettin' up in the mornin's concerned, It's
five thirty sharp. The bugle'll blow and I'll come around
with a big whistle to help you hear the bugle. For the

first coupla days you may have a little difficulty in
hearin' the whistle so I'll turn your beds over to signal
that the whistle has blown. Then yuh got six minutes
to dress and line up for reveille. It used to be five
but some college boys had it changed through
channels. Yuh got three months to get in shape
and I promise you when you leave here you'll
be hard as rocks from the cranium down. Got that?
Now go inside, locate your beds, get rid of your
gear and be back in five and a half minutes! And
anyone who isn't, report to the latrine and pick
out a mop! Yer in the army men — the sooner you
grasp that the better! Now — get goin'. Tetch-hut!
Yuh see . . yuh wasn't ready!

Princess by Birth

*An exiled Princess has grown into womanhood. She is
no fool. One may detect, however, a touch of sorrow
and some anger in the fact that she cannot return to
rule her small nation.*

Count Karak, please. Don't talk nonsense. You say
I am a princess but what am I a princess of? I do not even
remember my mother, much less my homeland. Be
patient — you tell me — for The Day. The Day. It will
never come, Count Karak — that Day. Really,
you are living in a fantasy — a pleasant one I know but
you must face reality. Princesses and dukes are a thing
of the past. Duchess is the name of my Pekingese. Please,
Count Karak . . don't make me laugh. Duty. Duty to
whom? My subjects? What subjects? Haven't you been
reading the newspapers? There is no Transylvania
anymore! They make cartoons about people like us and
our Holy Crusades! In any case I'd rather stay with
people I've grown to know and like. They would be
stunned if I told them I had a duty to my subjects.
They'd have me see a psychiatrist. Dear Count, I must
ask you to please try and discontinue these visits. I
have a jealous lover for one thing and he is very
suspicious. I can tell you something else — if you wish
us to be remembered as a great nobility I would suggest
you tell the newspapers what I told you — that the whole
idea of reinstating royalty in Transylvania is inspired by
bad cinema. Will you tell them that — for me? Count
Karak? Oh my dear, dear Count . . please don't cry,
or I shall have to summon the doorman.

23

Voice of Experience

*A youthful Iago tells a reticent friend how to win an
attractive young girl at a party. He gets carried away
by his own advice.*

Don't be timid Marvin. Just walk up to her and ask her
if she's free. If she says no that's it. If she says yes ask
her to dance. If she says all right — okay. If she says
she's not in the mood ask her how about a stroll in the
garden. If she says okay — okay. If she says she's
susceptible to hay fever tell her you are too but unlike
her you are willing to risk it because you find her so
temptingly intriguing. If she giggles you're in. If she
blushes that's a good sign. And if she says she doesn't
make a practice of walking in gardens with strangers at
parties you tell her you'd like to remedy that situation
at once and sit her down and do some fast talking. Keep
it light. Tell her you'd like to phone her some rainy
Monday and perhaps you could both go to a movie
or a hamburger place that's different. Make one up.
If she says good idea, you're in. If she turns you down,
well, then I'd say something that smacks of finality
such as "Okay I can take a hint." And if she says "Wait
a minute you've got me all wrong I really like you it's
just that I'm rather shy" well jump right in with "Great!
Because I'm shy too though you may not think it since I
did ask you if you were free but that was a reflex
action pure and simple because you're so temptingly
intriguing." If, on the other hand, she says she's
still not interested or "Please stop bugging me kid or
I'll call my brother the state trooper" well then Marvin
I'd throw in the towel. But for now . . at this stage of

1   *(contd)* the game I'd walk right up to her and ask her
2   to dance. What have you got to lose? You can't dance?
3   Look — you stay here. This girl's beginning to fascinate
4   me. *(Walks over to her)* I've been staring at you all
5   evening gorgeous. What do you say we ditch this dull
6   do and get some chili? Terrific. See you later Marvin.
7
8
9
10
11
12
13
14
15
16
17
18
19
20
21
22
23
24
25
26
27
28
29
30
31
32
33
34
35

24

Husband Killer

A woman in the prison laundry tells another inmate about how her marriage broke up. She seems resigned to her fate.

Night and day he stared at the tube. One T.V. set wasn't good enough for him — he bought six. Said it helped the economy. He had one T.V. set hangin' up over the bed. He even had one in the bathroom. The super had to run a special line into the fusebox. Five dollar tip. He had three color sets in the living room and he put 'em all on at once. On three sets three different shows. I went nuts watching him switch channels from one of them directors' chairs with his name on the back. I told him he was power crazed and that I couldn't take it anymore but he wouldn't listen. I began going to the movies just to get out of the house. Then one night I came home he's got on the All Star Football, The Roller Derby, and Joan Crawford all at once. He was on his second case of Millers. The movie I went out to see was lousy and I was depressed to begin with so when I was confronted with this sickening spectacle I took that iron dog he bought me in The Palisades Park and I killed him with his own gift. I sold the T.V. sets and flew to Miami but the cops caught me under an assumed name. I got six to ten. I would have got life but the lady judge took pity on me. In France I might have gone free. In Greece I would have probably got the chair. You know something? As soon as he bought that iron dog I knew there was gonna be trouble.

Executive Advice

A hard-hitting operator gives some advice to a young
fellow who's looking for a job. He double-talks him
to death.

That's the way Bill— keep plugging. And one day you'll
carve out a career in this ruthless jungle! But let up for
an instant and whoosh! You may bypass that opening
lurking in the haze — waiting for you — to reach out —
and take it! See people Bill! Relentless! Plug-plug-plug!
Not just me and Phil Hudson. We already like you!
See other people ! Important people! Haunt them!
Bother 'em! Pester 'em till they can't get your face out
of their morning Grape Nuts™ ! Push-push . . that's the
secret Harvey! It's also your one big problem. You're
too retiring. No room for modesty in our world today.
You gotta blow your own horn. God knows if you don't —
who will? What? Sure I believe in you Harvey! Christ —
you've sold me! But just me and Phil knowing you've
got the stuff means nothing! You've got to make an
impression on every big man in this street, and it's
a big street! Then when I mention you they'll say,
"Harvey Candleman, oh, yes . . a tiger-like gentleman with
a sure gift of gab." And you're in! So . . take Harry
Johnson out to lunch. He likes French food. And old
Wiley Finch . . he likes to booze — take him over to
Charlie O's. You two should hit it off beautifully.
After Wiley — Biff Sarazen. Get him a girl. For God's
sake, Harvey, don't count on me alone! You've already
won me! Another thing, kid . . don't mention my name.
It may seem like name-dropping and that's certain death
to job hunting. Put'er there, kid — and the best of luck!

Age Difference

An athletic girl is in love with rather a vain man fifteen
years her senior. Subconsciously, she isn't comfortable
with her situation.

Happy birthday darling! *(Kisses him)* Mmmwah!
Something the matter Milford? I've never seen a glummer
birthday boy. Don't you want to see what I got for
you? No? Ohhh .. poor Milford forty years young and
feels like an old man. It's all up here fella! Sylvester
was twenty-seven and he came on like sixty-five! He
actually fell asleep one night during dinner — in a
restaurant! It's all in the mind. Look at it this way
sweetie .. when you're a hundred and one I'll be
eighty-six. Now you're talkin' .. let's see those dimples ..
there's my Milford. When I told mother it was your
birthday she asked who was older you or my cousin
Truman. I'm not kidding. She thinks you're thirty-three.
What's wrong with thirty-three?! You sure you don't
want to see what I got you? Go ahead open it. I think
you're gonna like it. *(Pause)* Honey .. this is a designer
warm-up suit from Florence and I had to order it a
month in advance to get it in your favorite color —
oxford gray. What are you so miserable about? Hey —
wait a minute! You don't have to stamp all over my
gift! What is the matter with you today Milford! *(Pause)*
Hold it. Just wait one minute here. I think I've got
it. Just a hunch but does all this have anything to do
with last week's marathon? I mean since that day you've
been kinda down in the dumps. How stupid I've been —
that was the turning point. When I edged you out. Well,
honey you didn't beat me by all that much last year.

1 *(contd)* And the year before when we met . . you just
2 about nicked me at the finish line. Maybe, over the
3 long haul I'm a better runner than you are. In college
4 I ran the mile in 4:23 and won letters and I feel I'm
5 getting stronger all the time. And you're a fine runner
6 and a strong tennis player and all that but let's face
7 it in another ten years you'll have been around for half a
8 century. I didn't mean that Milford! Milford — come
9 back! Milford! Now what ever made me say a stupid
10 thing like that?
11
12
13
14
15
16
17
18
19
20
21
22
23
24
25
26
27
28
29
30
31
32
33
34
35

Impresario

A ballet master from the continent takes a certain
cruel satisfaction in lecturing a talented ballet dancer on
the facts of life in the world of the arts.

Yolanda Jones you were a sensation in St. Louis. Do
not let it go to your head. If you wish to be part of the
Ballet de Monte Carlo it isn't enough to possess a
certain amount of grace and good looks which incidentally
you do have. To spare I might add. A fringe member of
the ballet corps created by the immortal Diaghelev
must be an accomplished artist . . one must have arrived
you see. A tour de force in Grand Rapids Michigan may
impress the Mayor's wife but not me. In our company
Pavlova did walk-ons! The Ballet de Monte Carlo
performs in the great capitals of the civilized world
whose audiences are not hoodwinked by little girls from
Pasadena whose mothers call them ballerinas at the age
of seven. They have seen Nijinsky! And they know! You
have beaucoup de talent Yolanda Jones but if you are to
be a dancer you must be married to the bar! It is
gruelling work but after a few years perhaps things might
happen for you. Are you up to all this Yolanda Jones?
Oh — I have made you cry. However — I take it your
answer is yes. If it is — just nod. Good. Now . . your
hairy friend who watched you from the back of the
house with the silly grin and the strenuous applause —
get rid of him over the phone. And your mother —
she'll have to go too. Everyone will have to go. You
shall be a puppet — manipulated by your art. And me.
Is it worth it? If it is — just nod. I said nod! There's a
good girl. Always remember — I am the great Babushko!

45

28

Fatalist

*Reminiscing in a bar with a comparative stranger, this
woman recalls the most meaningful relationship of her
life. An introvert by nature she's resigned to taking
things as they come.*

I was in love once. He was a sailor. I'm not kidding.
He also used to paint. Pictures. They were beautiful.
Landscapes more often than not. But here and there he
did faces and people who were mostly in some kind of
trouble. At least that's the way I saw them. But he
didn't seem to care to discuss them. He said whatever
was up there on the canvas just was. And that they were
either good or not so good. I asked him why he didn't
settle down somewhere and just paint. He said he
couldn't afford to. That paints were expensive. I
told him to put in for a grant or something. He said
he didn't know how. And that anyway he loved
traveling. He always told me all about where he'd been
and now I feel as though I've been there too. We were
together three years and he went to sea every spring and
fall and once in the dead of winter. Mostly he'd go to the
Orient because it was a nice long deal and he could save
lots of money. That one winter he went to Indonesia and
I haven't heard from him since. A few months ago I
started to think of him a lot so I phoned the Merchant
Marine. They told me he's in England. They mentioned
something about his family being with him now. Well, he
wasn't English by any stretch so it can't be his uncle or
aunt. It's got to mean he got married and has a kid or
two. If I had the courage I'd write him but since
actually I didn't really fall in love with him until

46

1   *(contd)*   after he left me maybe it would be unfair . .

2   if I contacted him now. Don't you think? I mean

3   it's all in retrospect . . isn't it? This idea of "what if."

4   What if we got hitched and all that. It bores me to

5   death. Though he always said England's not the

6   place for it . . I hope he's still painting.

7

8

9

10

11

12

13

14

15

16

17

18

19

20

21

22

23

24

25

26

27

28

29

30

31

32

33

34

35

Fortune Hunter

A desperate young man senses the chance of a lifetime.
Marriage to an heiress. She may not be as foolish as he
thinks.

Why do I want to marry you. Well, Penny for one thing
I do love you. You are the most intelligent, charming
and gracious person I've ever met. You are the most
discerning, elegant woman I've ever yearned to kiss.
And you are the absolute antithesis of a mug like me
who has never been anything but a rogue, a ski-bum,
and a scalawag. Don't you get it, Penny? We're
opposites! And that is why we are bound to be ecstatic!
We've so much to give one another. You can teach me
to be industrious and considerate . . and I will teach you
how to play golf. Do you like golf? Well how about
tennis? You can teach me tennis? Well darling —
teach me tennis then! You see — I give in! No argument . .
and why not? I can trust you. Say you'll marry me,
Penny. I need you more than Romeo needed Juliet.
It was Juliet who needed Romeo? Interesting. You
see, already I'm learning things I never would have
dreamt about if I'd married Ethel, or Meredith, or
Joyce. What? Well Joyce is lying. I'd make a splendid
husband. Take me anywhere. I know you love to
travel . . and I am a wanderer from way back. Still I've
never really enjoyed myself in say Paris because I've
never shared it with anyone wordly — like you . .
to help me experience the hidden meaning of Rome . .
or Cairo or even Atlanta. What does Joyce know?
I'll bet she told you I was a fortune hunter. Did she
tell you that? Poor sweet thing. What some women

1   *(contd)* won't stoop to after they've been jilted. Let's
2   elope. Now. Tonight. I know a cute little judge in
3   Greenwich. He watches T.V. all night long . . stays
4   up for impetuous people. Where are you going Penny?
5   To wake up your father?! What do you want to do
6   baby — ruin everything?!

7

8

9

10

11

12

13

14

15

16

17

18

19

20

21

22

23

24

25

26

27

28

29

30

31

32

33

34

35

30

Cat Lover

A lonely somewhat mysterious woman rambles on about
cats. She strokes her cat possessively as she babbles about
the security she apparently lacks.

I can't remember when I did not have a cat. Cats are
peaceful and I love to hear them purr. They're much
wiser than dogs and they know it. They have
independence. Take Victor here. She's almost pompous.
Right, Victor? Ouch. Watch yourself, Victor. A dog
will do anything, just throw him a bone. A cat won't
be your slave. No, don't ever cross a cat. Isn't that
right Victor? Aatt's a girlee. Ooop . . don't scratch now.
She's really a boy but she's been taken care of. Listen
to her purr. Isn't it exquisite? I used to have two cats
but we lost Prince up in Canada. Didn't we, Victor?
On that trip we took. Prince was very self sufficient.
I found him in an alley. I took him home, bathed him
and gave him my own dinner. And he started purring
to beat the band. I wanted to have him taken care
of in Toronto and maybe he just sensed that and ran
away. Victor will never leave me because there's a
bond of mutual respect between us. She adores it when
I rub her neck. Don't you darling? Let's not be vicious
now. Every so often you rub Victor the wrong way
and she claws you . . but generally speaking cats are
peaceful little things. There's a good girl. Ouch!
You bitch! It's the he coming out in her now. I think
we'd better see that vet again.

31

Old Vaudevillian

*An ex-song-and-dance-man reminisces at a table at The
Lambs. He's a sentimental fellow but, in his own square
way, sincere.*

Oh, where are those great clowns of yore? Where's
Bill Fields and Willie Howard? Who's gonna take the
place of Will Rogers and Bob Woolsey and that peer of
all showmen, a jerk in person but a brilliant entertainer,
the immortal Jolie? *(Bursts into song)* Rockabye my
baybeee . . Who . . who's got it like they had it? Tell me
somebody, who's got it like Georgie Cohan had it? Over there
overr therre . . Nobody! Ted Lewis! *(Sings)* When my
babee smiles at meee . . It's a lost art. Those fellas had
class. They had an aura about 'em. Remember Bert
Williams? First satiric black man. And Sir Harry Lauder
with that crooked cane? Captured you in the first five
seconds. There was an aura about Harry . . a definite aura.
All of 'em had it. They'd get out there on the runway
or wherever the hell they were and didn't even have
to open their mouth. It was osmosis! Benny Fields!
(Sings) For I only have eyes for you . . and the fallen
sparrow Edith Piaf *(Sings)* Padampadampadam . . no one
knew what the hell it meant but she scored. Durante
and Wynn and little Bobby Clark. Did twenty minutes
on writing a letter. You do that today they blacklist
you. Bert Lahr and Sophie Tucker. *(Sings)* When my
baybee smiles at meee . . I mean *(Sings)* Some of these
dayyyss . . I could go on for hours but I hate to rattle
off names of dead people. Who me? Well I guess you'd
say I'm the last of the great ones. *(Sings)* Toot toot
tootsie goodbye . . I'm the only one holdin' the fort!
(Sings) California here I come! An I'm not ashamed to
get down on my knees either! Mammmyyyyy . . .

The Waiting Room

*A woman is terrified of the dentist. As she waits her
turn in the outer office she talks her heart out to a
stranger trying to read a magazine.*

Every time I get a whiff of outer office dentist I'm
through. How about you? The only reason I'm here is
my husband told me if I held off any longer I'd have to
pay the bill myself. Medicare doesn't cover dental
surgery does it? What's the difference — I'm only forty.
I admit it. I hate the sound of thirty-nine. It's phoney.
Ohh — do you hear that drill?! Brrr . . It's getting so I
can't stand back issue magazines. What are you reading —
Esquire? Gave it up — couldn't get it out of the letter
box. *(Pause)* I suppose it's different with a man. Then
again we go through childbirth. I'd like to see a guy in
stirrups. Still there are all types of men. Brrrwoww!
Hear it?! Still drilling. They should pull 'em out as soon
as they appear — the wisdom teeth — when you're young,
gay, carefree and don't give a damn. Hmm? *(Pause)*
Molars, bicuspids, fangs. The names alone. Brrrr . .
Listen to the drill . . bzzzzz. They got silencer guns,
why can't they invent a silencer drill? If I could only
relate to something else while I'm in the chair. Skiing.
Or recipes. Sex even. I have the same trouble on the bus.
Everyone stares at me and I get off. Here you're strapped
to the chair. Capital punishment. Even the X-rays gag me.
You suppose the water they schpritz on it does any
good? Nahh . . just a psychological ploy. Oh my you hear
it now?! I can just feel that hot metal instrument in my
mouth! *(Pause)* Oh nurse — this man fainted. You got
some water?

33

Hillbilly

This hillbilly gets all riled up when his wife tells him to
go to work. He's a lazy old hillbilly with no purpose in
life, but he isn't dumb.

How kin yuh talk like that Hester? Why don't I git
up off'n my tail an go to work. You know, Hester,
yuh sound as if I never done nuthin' in my whole life.
Well yer dead wrong about that. Dead wrong. When I
wuz younger me an' your old daddy set up the first
still in this here whole territory. The first still, mind ye!
My idea! Because I knew soon's they passed that there
wicked law them folks in the big cities'd pay fer
anything s'long as it burned the hell out of them when
it went down. Them was my days Hester. Proheebishun
they called it. But tuh us it was jes like we hit a vein o'
silver right here in Trout County. An' yuh know somethin
else? If not fer me yuh'd be dead tuhday Hester. Dead
as ole Ruppert Tyndall's mutt. An buried! Yuh don't
remember do yuh — you was a little girl an you was
sick an I hadda borry that ole Chevvy frum Hank
Perkins an ride allaway up tuh Charleston inna rain tuh
fetch that there genuine doctor Hellman or whatever the
hell he was called — yuh don't remember that, do yuh? Yuh
should remember — I saved yer life! Yuh had malaria!
An yuh know what I give him fer fixin' yuh up? A
jug o' corn liquor. The best! The kind yer daddy an'
I saved fer ourselves — an that there gangster frum New
Orleans. Took it?! He drank half of it sayin' goodbye!
An you got the nerve tuh tell ole Jake he oughta git up
off'n his buns an go tuh work. Hell no. I dun dun my
work — in my time — which was and is the proheebishun eı
Sure wish it was back agin. Wonder whut happened to that
there Doctor Hellman . . probably drank hisself tuh death.

34

Supermom

A former housewife turned executive phones her
unemployed husband who has taken over household chores
One gets the impression they are slowly drifting apart.

Hello . . is that you? Well, it's me. Me . . your wife . .
who'd you think it was — Meryl Streep? Look dear I
won't be able to make it home tonight. For dinner.
There's a meeting at seven and I've got to prepare for it
so put the casserole in the oven turn it up to 350 and
leave it for 35, 40 minutes. How's the little one doing?
Good. Don't forget to wake her at 6 and feed her some
applesauce. It's on the shelf next to the broccoli. In the
fridge! I hear lots of noise. The dishwasher? What do you
need to wash dishes for anyway before dinner? You're
practicing? Please don't talk that way Fred. It's just
a matter of time. You'll be right back on top. Think
positive. I know you're bored. You wanted to fire the
maid . . not me. So she took a few things, who cares?
Anyone who craves your old tieclip and those corny
socks with the clocks in them can have 'em. They're
coming back? I think your flipping out — they're coming
back. Look honey if you can't handle it we'll just have
to get another maid. We can afford it. We won't take a
vacation this year. I'll go up on the roof with a hose
or something. What do you mean you need one —
you've been on vacation for four months. I'm sorry I
said that Fred. And we'll definitely take a vacation this
year. We'll go to Paris but I've got to hang up now
because the boss is staring right at me. No I won't
tell him that. Remember, Fred, I didn't want to go
to work. You insisted I do and when I did you got mad.

1 *(contd)* Well I don't mind anymore . . in fact I like
2 it . . and I rather like my boss and if you don't stop
3 complaining and try to look at the sunny side of life
4 I'm going to have to do something about it. How do I
5 know? I swear you've got me edged right up to a
6 precipice Fred! One little shove now is all it's going to
7 take. Is that the baby crying? Oh it's you. I'm
8 terribly sorry Fred. I'm sorry I yelled at you but I'm
9 up against a deadline. You of all people should know
10 what that means. So feed yourself and little Donna
11 dear . . and I'll be home about ten-thirty . . make it
12 eleven. All right? Hello . . . *(He has hung up)*
13
14
15
16
17
18
19
20
21
22
23
24
25
26
27
28
29
30
31
32
33
34
35

Exasperated Customer

*Nerve-wracked and hungry he has been impatiently
awaiting some service. He finally gets the waiter's
attention but the latter's matter-of-fact attitude drives
him to distraction.*

Waiter. Oh waiter. Waiter! What the devil's the matter
with you? I've been shouting my head off for over half
an hour here. You're sorry? What have you been doing
back there — watching the ten o'clock news? All right
then. I'm ravenous. I haven't made up my mind yet!
Okay? I know I got the menu. What do you think I am —
senile? Let's see here — how's the chopped liver? Good
huh? I don't know why I'm asking you — what kind of
answer should I expect? Anyway I'm starving and I got
no time to argue . . so I'll take the chopped liver. Wait a
minute! Hold it! Where are you running to? I want you
to take my whole order now in case I never get to see
you again. Okay? Here we are — soup . . do I get soup?
If I pay for it? I mean is it on the dinner? Okay —
how's the vegetable soup? Good huh? Have you tasted
it? Then how do you know it's good? It was good
yesterday and it's the same soup. Only thicker. What
are we in Lindy's here? Make it chicken soup. Hold the
noodles. Now . . what have we here. Yankee Pot Roast
or frankfurters and beans. How's the Yankee Pot Roast?
What do you mean take the frankfurters and beans?
What kind of an answer is that? Look — I'm going
to call the manager. Now, for the last time . . how's the
Yankee Pot Roast? You never were a baseball fan? Wise
guy . . where's the boss? Watching the ten o'clock news?
Listen if I weren't starving I'd call the cops. So bring

56

1	*(contd)* me one chopped liver . . one chicken soup
2	hold the noodles . . frankfurters and beans . . apple pie
3	and coff . . okay custard. And tea with milk . . okay
4	lemon. But I'm going to tell you something in advance . .
5	No tip! And I want two glasses of water! Okay!?
6	
7	
8	
9	
10	
11	
12	
13	
14	
15	
16	
17	
18	
19	
20	
21	
22	
23	
24	
25	
26	
27	
28	
29	
30	
31	
32	
33	
34	
35	

Home Late

A girl comes home late and finds her mother waiting up
for her. She resents it but also realizes how lonely the
woman must be.

Well mother — now really! This is the limit! It's almost
dawn! Of course I was out with a man! Would you feel
better if I was out with a girl? I know I have to work
tomorrow. Have I ever been late for work? What are
you doing — watching television? What's on? Oh . .
Laurence Olivier. Why is it the best pictures are always
on at four in the morning? No mother . . I didn't go to
bed with anyone. I went to a party. Just a party . . drinking
and listening to records and talking and kissing. A party!
I'm a big girl now mother . . I've been married and
everything. I think I saw this picture. He ends up dead
on the deck and she winds up walking the streets. It's
sad. No I don't want any tea and cookies. Okay . . I'll
take an apple. I think she's married — isn't she? And
he comes back without an arm? For the last time
mother I did not go to bed with anyone tonight! I'd
like to have but I didn't! Now I remember — he's
married too. After he dies she ends up a prostitute . .
I think I saw it twice. What? No I like the skin. Don't
peel it please! Thanks. Avery — the boy you liked,
remember? The one with the checkered suit. Why
didn't I go to bed with him? He had to get home . .
his wife was waiting for him. What's the matter now —
I tell you the truth and you get all upset. Now, no tears . .
please mother . . I'll tell you what, let's have some tea and
cookies and we'll watch the ending together and we'll both
have a good cry together. Okay? That's better. You
know I must have seen this picture four or five times and
I'm still glued to it.

Skeptic

A little person attempting to be interesting. Something
of a snob in reverse, proud of his ersatz philosophy . . .
he may be reaching for something in a strange way to
justify his existence.

When I was a little boy I refused to believe there was such a
place as Albania. Only one in the class who wouldn't
buy it. Even though it was there on the map and we
answered questions about it in school I wouldn't
believe it. I still don't. Not until I see it . . until I feel
the soil of Albania under me. Right? Now I haven't
been to Albania yet and I don't ever intend to go and
therefore Albania hasn't, doesn't, and will never exist
for me. Call me a skeptic if you will . . I say show me.
Now that doesn't mean show me something in a book.
Right? I ask physical contact. T.V.? Newspapers?
That's all doctored. I don't even believe my best friends.
Call it a quirk but that's the kind of bozo I am. One of
the reasons I never bet on ballgames — unless I'm there.
Think I'm gonna take the word of some sportscaster
about who won? My guess is as good as his. *(Chuckles)*
About those fellows who say they climbed something
called Mount Everest. You believe that tripe?
Astronauts. Landing on the moon, so-called . . it's all
done to get people's minds off things! Right? World
War Two? I guess something went on over there but I
never left the states, so I can't say any actual "war"
took place. I didn't see any fightin'. How do we know
for sure it wasn't all part of a plan to give some
people other people's jobs while they joined the army.
Right? I'm talkin' skeptic man! What's that? Now

1	*(contd)* wait a minute . . that I believe! Why? Because
2	I saw one land in my backyard that's why . . and a little
3	guy with a high forehead come out and contacted me
4	and brought me greetings from the planet Loki . .
5	some three billion miles away. And he had seven
6	fingers on his left hand. Now this I witnessed! I
7	ain't never witnessed Albania!
8	
9	
10	
11	
12	
13	
14	
15	
16	
17	
18	
19	
20	
21	
22	
23	
24	
25	
26	
27	
28	
29	
30	
31	
32	
33	
34	
35	

Ex-Fall Girl

A girl who's been around. A two-timing ex-lover,
wounded in a scuffle with the police, knocks at her door
late at night.

What do you want Jerry? Come on Jerry it's four a.m.
No more craziness please. What's the matter? You look
like a ghost. Did you do something wrong? If you did,
go to your mother's house. If she'll take you the way
you treated her. I don't want any cops in here Jerry.
You look hurt . . are you hurt? Oh, the landlord's dying
for something — anything to get me out of a rent
control. You look bad Jerry. If you're in trouble, don't
come crying to little Irene cause she's had it with you.
Off the couch Jerry! Let's go — out. I'll call Charlie
with the Buick. They got Charlie?! What does that mean?
Jerry — you gotta get outta' here! Why do you always
have to give me a hard time? Are you drunk? Or what?
Oooo . . blood. That's just what I need now . . accomplice
to a murder. Perfect. Four bullet holes in his hat and
he takes a taxi straight to Irene. Let me see. Ooooo . .
Jerry it looks bad. I'm going to get a doctor. Okay?
I know a nice Jewish man down the block. He cured my
back . . gee Jerry don't die here! I wouldn't know what
to do . . or say. I got a new steady now . . and we're
serious. He's very jealous, Jerry. *(Dials)* Please stick
it out until I can get Doctor Silverman . . he's only a
few blocks away. All right Jerry? Jerry! Oh my God —
he's dead.

Prospector

*This old timer expounds upon his obsession for gold to
two tourists as he examines tray after tray for the real
stuff. He is a fanatic but a delightful one.*

It's gold I'm seekin' friends and you can laugh all you
want to. Just the way you see in them cartoons I'm
pannin' fer gold. Like the salesman says, "yuh gotta
know the territory." In here. *(Pats stomach)* It's all in
here. A gut feelin' for it. If you don't have that . .
itch . . and not just a simple greed fer riches . . then
play the horses or open up a business on some street —
but if the quest fer gold pure and simple takes you by
the craw there ain't much you kin do about it. There . .
see that? That's no good. Yeahp . . that shiny stuff it
looks nice but it's no good . . noo . . gives the amateur
a bit of a thrill that's all. Want a few nuggets? There
y'are help yourself. Chicken feed. What I'm after ain't
shiny at all. It's dull. Sometimes it's so dull it's
downright boring. But that's it see? That's the real
thing. Life's a little like that . . ain't it? *(Chuckles)*
Yeahh . . it's dull an it's heavy. Heavier than lead.
Most folks don't know that. And it's malleable, too . .
yess'r . . and when yuh git near it . . you kin smell it . .
if yer an old geezer like me. Here's some more of that
shiny stuff . . go head don't be bashful . . *(Spots
something in his tray)* give it to your nephew. Tell
him you met an old timer . . who remembers . . when
men used tuh kill fer gold. Today there's thousands
come up here . . on their vacations . . it's a game
to them . . nothing personal you understand. But I'm
deadly serious. I am gold crazy. I'm an artist!

1	*(contd) (He's really found it)* And I tell yuh somethin'
2	friends . . I smelll gollld! And you wanna know where
3	it's at? Oh that's all right I kin tell you . . you wouldn't
4	know it if you had it in yer hand! It's up there! In that
5	crevice longside the hill! And yuh know how I know?
6	Cause a minute ago I spot these five or six downright
7	boring nuggets and they're worth about six-seven
8	hundred dollars apiece as is — and here's three or four
9	more. And they're sure as sugar leadin' up to that hill
10	up there! Go head! Take all the photographs yuh
11	want of this crazy old man! *(Laughs hysterically as he*
12	*strikes some outrageous poses)* I'm gonna mine me some
13	gold! *(Laughs hysterically as he scampers up to the hill)*
14	
15	
16	
17	
18	
19	
20	
21	
22	
23	
24	
25	
26	
27	
28	
29	
30	
31	
32	
33	
34	
35	

40

Health Nut

This practical woman has finally had enough of her
husband's preoccupation with health. Underneath, she
wishes he were that concerned about her.

Sinus condition? You've got a cold dearie. A good,
old, bad cold. And all the mashed yeast, carrots and
beancurd in the world ain't gonna help. You've
succumbed to the bug baby and if you insist upon
going to work today you're liable to infect seven other
people and collapse at your desk. So stop trying to
slip into your baggy tweeds and take these two aspirins
and a tumbler of tea and mosey on into the guest room
because I certainly don't want to get what you got.
Sinus flare-up my ear . . come on open your mouth.
I said open your mouth! You mean that's as far as
you can go? Try and say ahh . . my God, no wonder . .
it's like gazing into Mount St. Helens. Just a little
sinus condition. What an ego. Wanna know what I think?
It may sound like heresy to you but . . eat a hamburger
for lunch once in a while instead of poppin' them
pollyseeds and alfalfa sprouts . . and don't jog in the rain.
The truth is that jogging's makin' you look like a
ghost. Do some push-ups or something that'll keep
you indoors in January. All that bull about not ever
having a cold in your life or a headache. You show me
a guy who's never sick a day in his life and I'll
show you a guy who's sick in the head! Even that
fella who played Patton had a sniffle and couldn't
go on the other night. Let's see — mhmm . . a hundred
and three and a half. You got the Borneo flu —
that's what you got! Take that coat off. You're not

1 *(contd)* goin' anywhere! No I won't get away from this
2 door. Try and push me away from it! Four to one you
3 don't have the strength to get on the bus! I wouldn't
4 kid you dearie. Your eyes are full of graffiti. You look
5 awful. Just go to bed, hmm? And I'll call the office.
6 All right I'll tell them it's a sinus flare-up . . sure . .
7 anything . . *(Dials)* just go inside. You want to listen?
8 Okay. . check up on me. Hello. This is Phil Kramer's
9 wife, Jocelyn. He won't be in today. He's got a sinus
10 flare-up, complicated by a touch of Borneo flu. *(Aside)*
11 Shut up. Well he forgot to eat his soyburger last night
12 and he thinks that did it. Yes . . I'll tell him. Thank you.
13 *(Hangs up)* Okay Superman, now get up and get in there
14 and I don't want to see you until Thursday!
15
16
17
18
19
20
21
22
23
24
25
26
27
28
29
30
31
32
33
34
35

Ex-Boxer

This punch drunk, battle-scarred veteran middleweight
is being interviewed by a sportswriter who specializes
in human interest stories. Tragi-Comedy.

Boxin' done an awful lot for me Phil. I . . I used tuh be
nuthin' but a bum. A bright bum maybe but a real
wastral. A punk. Yuh know what I mean? Boxin' took
me off the streets an put me indoors where I belong.
Fourteen years of punchin' it out with the best of 'em.
Mickey Walker . . Fred Apostoli . . I fought Slapsie Maxie
once. TKO inna third. No, he won but he knew I was
there. Now I can't speak so clear, can't see too good,
my hearin's impared and my brain's a little scrambled.
But I . . I become adjusted tuh society! Right Phil?
Whereas before I was nuthin' but a bum. I mighta taken
the wrong road — yuh understand? I coulda' become
a real criminal. But now . . now . . I . . I . . I . . better
get outta here Phil — I think I see a cop.

Girl with Odd Tastes

A working girl and her date in an ice cream parlor after
taking in a movie. They are both rather unconventional
types and happy with themselves. The girl rambles on . .
as she fondles the menu.

You know what? You got a funny face. Not funny
hysterical — funny way out . . almost freakish. Not that
I don't go for freak-like faces. Sometimes, a real offbeat
look excites me. For instance you wouldn't call the guy
in the movie tonight handsome would you? Yet he's a
star. Go figure it. What are you gonna have? Coffee-
pineapple sundae with the chopped filberts. Hmm. I
once met an architect with the strangest face you ever
saw. I've seen some weirdo heads on ordinary clerks
and tellers but this here architect . . he had a nose from
here to Columbus Ohio, bushy eyebrows, a big bottom
lip and cockeyes. And you know something, he was
sexy! Sort of a cross between Karl Malden and Prince
Charles. If you can picture it. I'll admit I was attracted
to him. Coffee-pineapple sundae with chopped filberts . .
eh? Maybe it's because I don't know there may be a
little of the freako in me. I get it from my mother
actually. Once she got lost at the circus and they found
her hiding behind a clothesrack in the ducklady's tent.
She was intrigued. Yeah, honey you got a real way
out feel. Wait till you meet my roommate. She's
another one with big eyes for off-the-wall guys. A
year ago she brought back a jockey and we made
dinner for him. He was about four foot tall. I knew
she wouldn't pull a mean joke just because the
guy was four feet tall to show him off. And sure

1   *(contd)* enough as it turned out she wasn't kiddin',
2   she really went for the guy, but it didn't last. She met
3   another oddball, a big ambulance driver with hairy
4   arms. Biggest goof you ever saw. I don't particularly
5   like gigantic men. You're more my type sweetie.
6   You're from outer space. Cuck-koo if you know what
7   I mean. *(Pause)* Oh . . I know. I'll have the Hungarian
8   Walnut Extravaganza . . with the mashed cherries . .
9   whipped custard . . and lots of fudge. And Miss . .
10   two slices of rye bread please . .
11
12
13
14
15
16
17
18
19
20
21
22
23
24
25
26
27
28
29
30
31
32
33
34
35

Psycho

A paranoid young man drives his date to a lonely
country road, turns into an area atop a cliff and stops
the car. He feeds on his companion's fear and then
chokes her to death.

Listen. It's raining harder. My father used to say rain is
a cleanser. You cold Bertha? Here, take my jacket.
There's nothing to be afraid of. I used to come here all
the time. When there was a real row at home — which
was almost every night. I'd sit and listen to the wind.
Goodness there isn't anything to be scared of. You're
just excited. We've never been alone together . .
especially like this. Miles from nowhere. Isn't it fun?
Please don't smoke with the windows closed Bertha.
That can be dangerous to the lungs. My mother always
lit a cigarette at breakfast. I couldn't take the smoke
with the cornflakes. What? Until the rain lets up.
If it ever does. What's the difference — right?
Don't try leaving me like that Bertha! Never do that
Bertha! Please! It makes me feel as though you
don't care for me one whit! My mother was a free
soul. She left . . for somewhere. I don't know where
the hell she is. Forgive my language but I have strong
feelings when it comes to family ties. *(Sighs)* The sound
of the wind coupled with the rain always had an
effect on me. Funny. And please don't cry! It makes
me uncomfortable. My father cried every night for
weeks but she never even sent a postcard. And it
won't do any good screaming Bertha — there's no one
up here. That's what makes an evening like this unique.
Bertha! That will do no one any good! If you do not stop I'll

1	*(contd)* be forced to take certain measures I'd rather
2	not take. Hands off the door! There. I really do not
3	relish chasing after girls in storms. For the last time —
4	no screams . . no yells . . and no stupid attempts to run
5	out on me and my conversation . . which, if I have to
6	say so myself, is way above the average Bertha! I'm
7	not some simple soul slaving over a greasy hamburger
8	griddle like my father . . wearing that idiotic white
9	buddy cap. I'm going to be famous some day soon and
10	then let's see how hard you struggle to break away and
11	call it a night! Honestly — just when the fun's starting . .
12	*(Pause)* Oh Bertha . . now you see what you made me do . .
13	
14	
15	
16	
17	
18	
19	
20	
21	
22	
23	
24	
25	
26	
27	
28	
29	
30	
31	
32	
33	
34	
35	

Home is the Tourist

This housewife has just returned from a trip to Europe with her husband who was there during the war. She tells some lady friends at tea about their time in Paris.

George had been in Paris during the war and he read
some books on it I guess and naturally he was a little
blase about everything. I remember we were sitting
in one of them cafes . . da Floor or something. Well
George had a few of the pernods and he started yelling
"Where's Hemingway?!" I imagine he meant the author.
"When I was here in 1940," he says, "Hemingway was
always sitting right there! Where's Hemingway?!" He
talked real loud, you know, and everyone turned around
and said to themselves — another drunken American
tourist. Happily most of them were American tourists,
too. Well anyway I was real embarrassed but far be
it from me to tell him he was a laughing stock. He'd
go on to Italy by himself and stick me with the hotel
bill. So I just sat there and as they say just grinned and
beared it. I'll never forget we were in The Louvruh
one day and we passed the beautiful Mona Lisa, and
take it from me girls it is gorgeous! Well, there's a
bunch of them foreigners standin' in front of it with
a guide, one of them Swiss or Dutch men. I couldn't
figure out what he was talking about but he sounded
interesting anyway. You know how those things usually
go. Well, as I was saying, we couldn't see the picture
because of the crowd standing right in front of it.
George didn't like that and I don't mind tellin' you
he had had a few, so he starts yelling, "Fake! It's a
fake! I know all about that phoney painting! It's a

1 (contd) fake!" Just like that, real loud. It's a fake!
2 Well, I tell you I could have hid myself inside an olive
3 I felt that big. Every one of them Finns or whatever
4 they were looked straight at us and George just stood
5 there laughing his head off. As you can imagine I felt
6 terrible. Well, about four or five of them floorwalkers
7 there just ushered us out kind of politely, but firmly,
8 as they say, and George wanted his money back. You
9 gotta pay for museums over there, you know. Like
10 New York. Well, there was one more thing that happened
11 in Paris before we left that I really shouldn't tell you
12 but if you promise not to tell George. You Promise?
13 Okay. One day George went out lookin' for one of
14 them black market men to change his money and they
15 took him in an alley and gave him a big pack of paper
16 in a rubber band with a ten franc note on top to make
17 it look good. He lost over five hundred dollars. Don't
18 ever tell him I told you or he'll beat my brains out.
19 Imagine five hundred dollars in travelers checks and
20 bills and he tried to get away so fast he left all those
21 jams and jellies behind for good measure. I tell you,
22 I may have a mean streak in me somewheres but when
23 he got back to the hotel with that package of toilet
24 paper with Napoleon on top I bust out laughin'. I
25 told him not to go in the first place but he'd never
26 listen to me. "I been here before! I know all about
27 it!" That was his trump card. Well, I tell you, I was
28 the happiest American ever to leave Paris. And it
29 was all because of George. Just because he'd been in
30 Paris during a war he acted like he owned the place!
31
32
33
34
35

Small Businessman

This man runs a lobby stand in an office building on Wall Street. He lives in the past but even so can't take it much longer. The thing that saves him is that he is somewhat of a philosopher.

I been behind this stand forty years now. In this self same office building which has won many prizes in its day for cleanliness and architecture. I seen 'em come and go. Bankers. Lawyers. Podiatrists. You name 'em I seen 'em. Come and go. Mostly go. In those days we carried a great cigar. They called 'em genuine Havanas. From Havana Cuba. They'd crinkle for a year or so after you bought 'em. Music to the ears of a true tobacco worshipper. Which there were millions of years ago. Today everyone's on dope. Not only the kids — the old timers too. They give up cigars on accounta' this here Castro. I figure if Castro woulda' lost they'd all be still smokin' them Havanas. And I wouldn't have to rely on Barbie Dolls and sick posters for a livin'. The other day I sold some El Banderos from across the border in Costa Rica — they fell apart in the guy's hands. Hadda make a refund. I'm no commie but unless we recognize Cuba mark my words the day of the cigar is over. I mean along with the cigarette scare how do they expect the small business man to survive? Still, maybe it's meant to be . . I don't know. A lot of institutions vanish. Never come back. Take your trolley car. Only the other morning guy comes over and asks for raspberry drops. I said how about lemon drops? He says raspberry. I said how about some licorice drops? He says raspberry. I told him . . look fella . . Raspberry's dead.

Professional Mother

A very social lady tells a weekend house guest how she is
responsible for the genius of her ten year old son.

Frankly he scares me Phyllis. I nursed him for a full
year. I dressed him when he was a boy. After DePinna
went — everything straight from Saks. I taught him to
speak French. I gave myself to him completely, and
now at the age of ten, Gerald frightens me! You've
never seen a child so engrossed in the latest scientific
data. He's obsessed with the world of the Arts.
Athletics leave him cold . . only yachting and lacrosse
make the slightest impression on him. But music!
He sits and listens to Bach for hours! Imagine!
Hindemuth . . Mozart . . Bartok he says relaxes him!
What's he going to be when he grows up? I've asked my
myself that question hundreds of times and the answer's
always the same. I just don't know Phyllis. I asked
Gerald yesterday and you know what he did? He
looked at me straight in the eye, kissed his forefinger,
put it to my forehead and said, "Please don't worry
your pretty little head about it mama." That — from a
boy of eleven! Ten. For all I know he is liable to wake
up one morning and say "Mother, I think I may just
have found the cure to the common cold." And wouldn't it
be something if he did! Yes, there are times when I
wish he were like other children but I guess it is
impossible to undo what has already been done. Don't
you agree Phyllis? *(Pause)* What's that Phyllis? How
the hell do I know what's good on television tonight! The
Late Show!

Flim Flam Man

*The banks want some references and a bit of background
before it loans some money to this fast-talking character.
He rambles on confidently, imaginatively, a happy-go-
lucky and personable fellow.*

New York was fine but between you and me I prefer it
out here. Oh, I worked in Wall Street. Good salary . .
private limo . . ten to four . . expense account . . but,
somehow, I got tired of it. Mind if I smoke? So I
went into the restaurant business with this chap I
met at Yale. Millionaire. We opened a little bistro
on 76th Street. East naturally. Had a sommelier . .
you know the guy with the chain and the wine card . .
the works. All a la carte. But after a bit I got bored
with that too, so I let my partner buy me out and I
went into cable television . . servicing Jersey City and
the New England area. Put on hit plays . . news
specials . . the top music talent . . got all the celebrities
to appear on my own interview show . . "Talk To Me,
Baby." Original isn't it? Which incidentally became
very popular and was finally syndicated. Well, mostly
in Canada . . Europe . . Japan . . Then I couldn't take
that for very long . . too much talk too little action . .
know what I mean? So I went on an oil-drilling
expedition in Yucatan with a few friends. The other
three fellows couldn't take the water so they left but
I stayed on and when I hit pay dirt so to speak everyone
remotely connected with that venture got his share
including my two Mexican dredgers. Then I did
something I always wanted to do. I flew to Paris
and bought up all the good art I could lay my hands

1   *(contd)* on . . set up shop in the Avenue Matignon
2   and made a potful of francs. Swiss. Oh, modern stuff
3   mostly . . abstract. No call for it out here but it's big
4   back east. And then . . finally . . I came to my senses.
5   Decided I'd sown enough wild oats and it was time to
6   settle down to something serious. That's why I want to
7   open this private detective agency right here in San
8   Diego. What I want to know is if you could stake me
9   to ten or fifteen thousand bucks so's I can start in a
10   month or so. I plan to have two or three on staff and
11   we're mainly concerned with — what? Oh didn't I
12   tell you I lost everything at Monte Carlo. Like the
13   man says easy come easy go. References . . well, I
14   may be able to get you my two dredgers . . but they're
15   scattered all over the place. Er . . how about the sound
16   engineer who worked on "Talk To Me, Baby?" I
17   believe he's located somewhere in Venice. California
18   that is. Well . . there's no harm in tryin' . . I always
19   say. You don't have a cigarette on you do you? I'm
20   out.
21
22
23
24
25
26
27
28
29
30
31
32
33
34
35

Advice to the Lovelorn

A small apartment in the slums. A woman irons a dress as she lectures her daughter. A family without a father.

It's eleven thirty already. You ought to be ashamed of yourself Hester . . lollin' around the house on such a gorgeous day. Go out. Take a walk in the park or somethin'. Look for a job. Do somethin' instead of hangin' around your room like a mope. Thank God your father, may he rest in peace, is spared the agony of watching you fritter away your youth indoors. If you stayed out till five a.m. I could see it . . but you went to sleep right after Merv Griffin. What intrigues you so about this place? What is it — a museum? There's nothing beautiful here! Take a walk to the zoo. Stand in front of the monkeys. They always draw a crowd. Did you hear about Fanny Armstrong? She found a wonderful guy in the subway of all places. He offered her his seat, she refused and they started a spirited conversation . . just like that. Who do you expect to meet hangin' around here — the Con Ed man? He's married and got three kids and a wife. That's the girl . . get dressed . . put on that taffeta print and you'll feel better. Take a nice stroll on such a pleasant day. Even if you don't meet anybody . . that's it . . it'll do you good just to get out and communicate a bit with nature. And Hester . . don't stay in the park too long. I hear all kinds of strange types wander around near the seals. Then again nowadays you're not even safe in your own home. Oh . . bring back a quart of milk and some tomatoes.

Prison Break Leader

This steely-eyed lifer discovers one of the men involved
in a carefully planned prison break has gotten cold feet.
One gets the feeling the hesitant con is in hot water.

You asked to come in on this Shorty. You volunteered.
You knew in advance we might have to waste a few
people and now you get second thoughts. That don't
register too good with Barney and Hank here. They
don't want any weak links. The question is — what
are we gonna do with you now? Do we just say okay . .
fine . . we still got a few minutes to get someone else?
Like Joey Taylor if he wants to come? Too late, Shorty.
The boat's sailed kid. We're in this up to our eyeballs.
The plan's been finalized since two days now. You
were there. In this same exercise yard over in the corner
you said "Okay . . no sweat" I think you said . . or
"no problem" I forget which. Maybe I shoulda'
stuck with my instincts then. When somebody says
no problem or no sweat there's usually lots of problems
and plenty of sweat. Because it's a stupid thing to say
especially about a prison break in a top-security,
break-free joint with screws comin' out of your ears
and cannons everywhere. Tell yuh what Shorty,
instead of you takin' care of McGuire while Hank
backs up the truck we'll give that chore to Barney.
And since you're kinda nervous you stick close to me
as I break through the kitchen. Very close cause I
might want to use you as a shield. How does that grab
you? Good . . cause we got about fifteen minutes till
our last breakfast on the house at this school of hard
knocks. What are you lookin' so worried about Shorty?
No problem.

50

At the Switchboard

The monotony of working all day at the switchboard is relieved somewhat by the boss' philanderings. This woman, experienced in her job, is actually a lonely person who lives vicariously.

Wingate Frocks, good morning. Mr. Wingate's not in. May I take a message? Thank you. It's her again. That fake voice. She tries to change it every time. *(Imitating)* Hello — is Mr. Wingate in? Tell him Miss Diane Hunter called. Of Hunter Knitwear. Wednesday, it was Miss Hattie D'Orsay of Bloomingdale's. Wait till this idiot's wife finds out. Wingate Frocks, good morning. Miss Tashman? Just a moment. Wait till she finds out about those trips to Vegas. Wow — what fireworks! She'll kill him. Wingate Frocks — good morning. I'm afraid you've got the wrong number. Sounds like a pervert. And she's crazy about him. How do I know why? He may be a great lover. He's certainly had lots of practice. Hello? Eleven-twenty-six. After all she's got some stake in him. She's his wife. Wingate Frocks. No, Mrs. Wingate he's not in just now. Yes, I'll tell him just as soon as he arrives. Thank you Mrs. Wingate. Such a lady! He doesn't deserve her! The monster and the saint. It never fails. Ooops — here comes Casanova. Your wife called Mr. Wingate. Said she'll meet you at the theater. And a Miss Bara phoned. Miss Bara said you would know where to get her. By the way did I give you that message from Miss Hunter yesterday? Just checking. See how white he got? He's really sleazy putting horns on a woman who stuck by him through shortages, operations and crazy in-laws. Wingate Frocks

1   *(contd)* good afternoon . . I mean Good Morning
2   Wingate Frocks. I don't know what I'm doing anymore.
3   Mr. Wingate? Yes . . who shall I say is calling? Miss
4   Turnbull of Turnbull and Asser? Go ahead Miss
5   Turnbull. *(Winks)* He must have a list of names she
6   gave him. *(Pause)* Richard Burton's playing at the
7   86th Street tonight. You want to go Doris? We'll
8   have dinner at the Brocherie or something. Hello . .
9   Wingate Frocks . . just a moment . . I'll see . .
10
11
12
13
14
15
16
17
18
19
20
21
22
23
24
25
26
27
28
29
30
31
32
33
34
35

51

Old Salt

*The town character. He's probably never been to sea but
actually believes he has. He fascinates a small boy with
tall tales of the briny deep in this New England
whistlestop.*

When I first set out to sea I was a lad your age. Can't
do that today. Against union rules. Our ship was called
The Esmeralda and the crew was as rough a bunch of
sea dogs as you'll ever read about. We went places like
Valparaiso, Bilbao and Gilbraltar with all them monkeys
jumpin' around . . and Hong Kong. Got a suit made there
for three dollars an fifty cents. Yess'r. There was
Cruikshank . . he was our first mate. Important job
laddie, first mate. Old Crookie was a Yorkshireman by
birth as big an brawny an foulmouthed as any pirate
that ever lived. But beneath all that blusterin' was a
heart of gold. Not so Bellows . . he was our bo'sun. He
had so many tatoos he blended with the sea. And he
was tough. He'd try mutiny just fer the fun of it. I
remember one night off the Cape O' Good Hope Bellows
got drunk as a mongoose and he an two other lads
broke into the Capun's cabin as a lark — tuh scare him!
They were sure a sight in three witch doctor masks. Well
just as they reach the Capun's door the old man himself
comes back from a brisk tour o' the deck — he couldn't
sleep, yuh see, worryin' about the cargo . . a load o' guns
fer the Boers in that there Boer War. Well the two lads
get cold feet an run . . but not old Bellows. He just
stood there in that wild mask and screams Boo! Right
in the old man's kisser! He got ten days in the brig and
busted down to ordinary seaman. That's how I got to

1	*(contd)* be bo'sun. That's sort of a top sergeant. Ah
2	laddie . . they was fine days on the old Esmeralda.
3	That's why I'm tellin' yuh . . even though the merchant
4	marine ain't near whut it was in my day . . although I
5	still think they got them salt water showers gotta get
6	a special soap tuh get clean . . it wouldn't be amiss fer
7	you in a couple o' years to sample a hitch in it. It'd
8	toughen yuh up and yuh'd sure get some livin' done
9	instead o' hangin' around this old burg waitin' for that
10	job in the laundromat tuh materialize. Take an old
11	salt's advice. You won't regret it. Oh-oh there's your
12	mother. Mind yuh don't tell her about our little chat.
13	
14	
15	
16	
17	
18	
19	
20	
21	
22	
23	
24	
25	
26	
27	
28	
29	
30	
31	
32	
33	
34	
35	

52

Professional Returner

She is street wise and precocious and bulls her way to
the complaint desk demanding a refund on a suspicious
item. For a time she has the psychological edge but she
gets carried away.

Look, I'd like to get my money back on this — okay?
I've been waiting over half an hour! They sent me to
the wrong desk. Naturally I've got a receipt. I had the
receipt. Just a minute. No . . I don't have a charge
here . . but I think I do have a receipt . . unless . .
unless . . you see it was a gift . . for my aunt. And people
usually don't give you a birthday gift with a receipt
attached to it. It isn't chic. That's the reason I don't
have the receipt — okay? I know it's not in the original
wrapping. So what? Anyone can pull that old trick.
Those are the people you have to watch honey not me.
I told you it was a gift to my aunt from a very dear
friend of hers. Does she have a charge here? My aunt?
Oh her friend. It's a he. It's possible. And then again who
knows. Okay? No I won't give you his name . . then
you'll tell him and he'll find out my aunt sent his gift
back. No I don't trust you — okay? Will I take credit?
No I want a refund I thought that was clear. Hold it . .
that sweater has not been worn! My aunt tried it on once and
I tried it on . . other than that it has not been worn! My aunt
decided she didn't like the style or the color. Besides she's got
four sweaters just like it and and she doesn't like them
either. That's her business. She always buys what she
hates. It's psychological. She hated her father. He
was in knitwear. You're confused? So am I honey. I'm
really mixed up. The biggest department store in the
world and you give customers a hard time when they

83

1	*(contd)* want to return a lousy 150 dollar cashmere
2	sweater. May I see the manager? You are the manager?
3	Okay — I'll take the credit.
4	
5	
6	
7	
8	
9	
10	
11	
12	
13	
14	
15	
16	
17	
18	
19	
20	
21	
22	
23	
24	
25	
26	
27	
28	
29	
30	
31	
32	
33	
34	
35	

Baseball Fan

This man fancies himself an authority on baseball.
He talks to everyone and anyone while watching the
game from the grandstand. Extrovert.

Watch. Watch the way he's fakin' it towards third. Watch.
I bet he breaks for third. What'd I tell yuh! Lookit him
sail! Beauty in motion! He's out! *(Pause)* Tryin' to
steal third on Johnny Bench . . he oughta have his head
examined. With that gorilla arm he's got you by five steps
before you start. I wonder who give him the order to
go. Some slob coach buckin' for manager. I forget who's
up next already lookin' at that dumbo tryin' to steal
third on Bench. Remmick? He's a new guy. I like his
style. Holds the bat nice an' high you notice? Strike one.
He takes a good cut. Watch. If he ever lays into one
it's bye bye birdie . . watch. Strike two. Well he's a
kid yet. A little anxious but if he ever polaxes one —
strike three . . swinging. Crazy sandlot bum. Swingin'
on a two and O count against Gibson. He ought to
surrender his brain to science right after the game. How
many outs is it? I forget how many outs it is I got so
interested in that there new kid Remmick. He stinks.
Oh here comes the big guy. Forty-five homers.
Number forty-six comin' up. Come on you big goomba,
hit it! Ball one. Lettin' the bad ones go by. He ain't
in no rush to go down swingin' like that bum Remmick.
Come on — lay into one Phil! Ball two. That looked
good. Lettin' the good ones go by. Jerk. Ball three . .
way outside. Two out — one run behind. If it's down
the alley he'll put it away. Watch. Tear the cover off
it Phil! Here it comes. What did I tell yah? Lookit

1 *(contd)* it travel! That's gone. ferget it. That's outta
2 here! Did you see that catch!? That big dumbo!
3 Three and O and he swings at it! A walk ain't good
4 enough for him! With number four batter up next!
5 He has to try and put one away. Showboat! What
6 inning is it now? Game's over? I'll take the little
7 leagues.
8
9
10
11
12
13
14
15
16
17
18
19
20
21
22
23
24
25
26
27
28
29
30
31
32
33
34
35

Shattered Dreams

They met as students in Paris. They married and
settled down in the big city. Their youthful dreams
have come to naught driving this woman to the brink.

No, William. I honestly don't care much for country
pine at the moment. I know. I know it's all the rage but
I'll not go out and hang myself if we make do without
it. Yes . . I've heard. Oriental rugs are in. But so is
lynx . . and lynx doesn't send me . . it may send us to the
poorhouse but that's something else. And you can take
those china dishes which are also in . . and bust them
over your mother's head. Oh . . I'm sorry William but
when we got married we planned to live in a loft on
Bleeker Street with wicker furniture and a broken down
piano and paint and have little parties with friends. Now
all I see are execs and contacts and financial wizards who
mull over every sip of wine as though we've committed
some terrible gaffe. Tell me what's the good of the
ottomans and the pouffes and chaise longues if we still
can't relax! You know something? Last night I dreamt
about our old barber's chair with the torn leather seat.
When I think you actually donated it to the Salvation
Army! You should have given them that marble
coffee table that weighs a ton. And I'm telling the
frame man to stop with the frames. I don't care if your
boss recommended him. I just found out he is robbing us
us blind. Who ever heard of frames costing more than
the paintings. Do you realize for the money we're
throwing away to keep up a front we could be living
on the Riviera? It's your dream isn't it? And now we
can't go because we bought a hutch for the kitchen!

1   *(contd)* And I can't go to the hairdresser this month
2   because I put a deposit down on a set of Gucci
3   ashtrays. And when last summer you said we could
4   go to Maine if we found a buyer for our sectional sofa . .
5   I must confess, William, that drove me to the wall. I
6   should have told you all this before? Why, William?
7   Is it too late?
8
9
10
11
12
13
14
15
16
17
18
19
20
21
22
23
24
25
26
27
28
29
30
31
32
33
34
35

Folk Singer

A young folk-singing star tells a group of sycophants
all about himself. A portrait in homey egomania.

To tell the truth I never took a lesson in my life. Jes'
lucky that way I guess. Must have had a great aunt who
had song in her right to her toes. When I was eight I was
singin' in barrooms fer nickles and dimes. An when I
was fourteen I wrote "Wanderin." Jes plain "Wanderin'" . .
cause it's got meanin' that way. If yuh care to ponder
on it. *(Sings)* Wanderin' . . wanderin' . . wanderin' . . all
over this great countree. Cities 'n towns. Ups or downs.
Smiles or frowns. Couldn't care less effen the world's
in a mess . . When you're wanderin' . . wanderin' . .
wanderin' . . It ain't heavy stuff but there's a message
there effen yuh care tuh hunt fer it. My biggest hit as
you all know is called "Driftin.'" Jes plain "Driftin.'"
Driftin's different from "Wanderin.'" When yuh wander
yuh're a little more uptight than when yer driftin'.
When yuh drift man yuh jes drift. Like it says in the
song. Which by the way sold over 5 million records.
And tuh my mind it's much more mature in concept
than "Wanderin.'" An altogether different feelin' here.
It goes *(Sings)* Driftin' . . driftin' . . driftin'. Out there
on that great prairie. Trees 'n sand. Lakes 'n land. When the ole
sweatband's around yer head. Couldn't care less
effen yer alive or dead . . Cause yer driftin' . . driftin' . .
driftin' . . Thank you . . thank you . . My next tune?
Well I'm workin' on somethin' in an altogether different
vein now. Little more ambitious I guess . . an I hope
I can pull it off. It's kinda a new concept in folk-
singin'. It's called "Rovin.'" Jes plain "Rovin.'"

1   *(contd)* Okay . . if yuh pass those albums over
2   I'll autograph 'em for you . . anybody got a ballpoint
3   or somethin'? I can keep it? Good. Rovin' . . rovin' . .
4   rovin' . . out there in the ole Outback . . .
5
6
7
8
9
10
11
12
13
14
15
16
17
18
19
20
21
22
23
24
25
26
27
28
29
30
31
32
33
34
35

Incessant Smoker

This couple has been married too long. She smokes too much and he's literally a closet drunk.

What is a crime? It's a habit. A crazy nervous habit. And it keeps me thin. You ought to thank God I do smoke you'd be embarrassed to walk in the street with me. I'd gain 8 pounds the first week. Suicide? You're nuts. You believe all those reports? What cough — it's a tickle in my throat due to nerves. Think of your throat better. Stop "soothing" it so much. You know what I mean. Don't play dumb. I see you creeping into your walk-in closet every hour on the hour in search of a little refreshment. I got eyes. And don't give me that clogging of the chest routine. Take some Gatorade.™ Yeah — I notice you look sick. I also notice how every day the bottle gets lower and lower and suddenly there's a full one again. You ought to thank your lucky stars I don't drink! Talk about money for cigarettes! If I drank we'd be paupers! A cigarette once in a while *(Coughs)* it's a nervous habit *(Coughs)* brought on probably by your drinking if you'd care to analyze it. You want me to grow into a hippo? Maybe you should go out and get a job. It'd get your mind off my smoking. *(Coughs)* There he goes . . into the closet again . . the lost weekend.

Dorm Eulogy

*An emotional college student upbraids his peers for their
inexcusable lack of positive action in an emergency
involving a celebrated professor.*

A demeaning way to go wasn't it? Among other things
he once won the Nobel Prize. And you're all standing
around chatting about who's doing it to who as this
great man with whom we are privileged to discuss life
with every day, battles for breath . . trying to force a
smile so as not to alarm anyone. I wouldn't be surprised
if you still think it was . . one of those things . . none
of your business. This cultured gentleman who had more
class in his pinky than any of you could conjure up in
a lifetime isn't around anymore because you were too
busy rapping to lend a hand in what any child would
sense was a dangerous time. I don't understand. Weren't
you at all curious? Or perhaps you felt it was beneath
you to ask whether he needed any help with his coat and
galoshes. Surely a genius should be able to handle that.
I realize it is fashionable not to be in awe of anyone
or anything. That's just not "in" today — awe. I mean
simple respect is suspect. And the Nobel Prize is rigged
anyway . . we all know that. So you watch this . .
this terrific guy of eighty fighting for his life and you're
making cracks "Oops looks like the old man's hit the
bottle again." And while you're chuckling and lighting
up he dies in the hall. And if I hadn't come along to
investigate he might be lying there yet. Well I am very
much in awe of Professor Werner Buchholz. And I've
got a very strong ego. Try me sometime. *(Pause)* Or —
were you all . . just scared?

92

Comedy and Comedians
Ramblings by-the Author

"Comedy? You either got it or you ain't," observed ten-percenter Phil Fields, or Furtive Phil as we used to call him in the old days, and for once he was right. Not every actor has a funny bone. The script can help but there is a vast difference watching a "comedien" as the French prefer to call their favorite actors, tackle Cyrano as compared to a competent straight actor playing the same part. One must possess an innate sense of fun and more than a little irony in his soul to get through those lengthy if beautifully written passages.

Cary Grant has a funny bone. Remember "Bringing Up Baby"? So does Maggie Smith. So do Marcello Mastroianni, Burt Reynolds and Ralph Richardson. And Angela Lansbury, Peter Falk, Michael Caine, Walter Matthau, Ugo Tognazzi, and Lucille Ball. Edith Evans was as funny as anybody. Alistair Sim was an original. Peter Sellers had comedy in his toes.

I doubt, however, that any of these performers with the possible exception of Peter Sellers could get up "in one" and hold an audience the way Jack Benny did — or Richard Pryor, Joan Rivers, Robin Williams and Don Rickles can.

Then again what standup comic can match the great "comedien" Laurence Olivier's magnificent clowning in Sheridan's "The Critic" — to say nothing of his spectacular tragi-comic portrayal of Archie Rice in "The Entertainer."

Mae West told a friend of mine her ultimate ambition was to play Lady MacBeth. And she wasn't kidding.

When Bertolt Brecht was asked whom he would cast as Mother Courage in America he said Mae West. He meant playing that pipe-puffing canteen keeper and camp follower with just a hint of sentimentality would wreck the play, distort its meaning.

Brecht was terrified of the average actor's inability to resist giving a "sympathetic performance" in plays of comment. I understand, on his death bed, Brecht mumbled mumbled, "Please . . don't let . . my wife (Helen Weigel) . . or Lotte (Lotte Lenya) . . direct . . any of my plays."

"Theater consists in this: making live representations of reported or invented happenings between human beings and doing so with a view to entertainment. Pleasure is the noblest function we have found for the theater." Who said that, George Abbott? Preston Sturges? Wrong. It was Bertolt Brecht.

"If you're going to scold the audience better make them laugh or they'll kill you." — Bernard Shaw

Charlie Chaplin, Buster Keaton. W.C.Fields, Fernandel, Laurel and Hardy, The four Marx Brothers, Louis Jouvet, and Bert Lahr are my golden dozen. They are great in the same way Matisse is great. No matter what any-body thinks. And John Gielgud in "The Importance Of Being Ernest" on stage was absolutely peerless despite the fact that the critics agreed. And Woody Allen is Freud's answer to Buster Keaton.

Jazz and slapstick. Two artistic contributions from America to the world. Isn't it infuriating to come across the critic's chestnut "from then on the play or film degenerated into sheer slapstick." Bad comedy perpetrated by unfunny people under the guidance of a humorless or pretentious director is another matter. But I for one would rush anywhere to watch sheer slapstick.

Humbolt's ravings in "Humbolt's Gift" had me screaming into the night.

Albums with staying power are "Beyond the Fringe," "The Best of Sellers," "Noel Coward in Las Vegas," and "Guys and Dolls."

Films I could see every month are "City Lights," "Seduced and Abandoned," "A Night at the Opera," "I'm All Right Jack," "The General," and "Big Deal on Madonna Street."

"Let me point out that one encounters tragedy in life, but life itself is not necessarily a tragedy." — Sean O'Casey

Superb characters who were natural comedians: Charles Coburn, Akim Tamiroff, Josephine Hull, Frank Morgan, Wallace Beery, Edna May Oliver, Sam Levene, Mary Boland, Barry Fitzgerald, Edward Everett Horton, Felix Bressart, Clarence Kolb, Sig Ruhmann, Charlie Ruggles, Sidney Greenstreet, and Eugene Pallette.

"You can't play comedy unless a circus is going on inside you." — Lubitsch

It's sad to see so many clowns who haven't a clue. I'm told there's even a school for clowns. Because somebody puts on a red nose doesn't necessarily make him funny. *"You either got it or you ain't." — Furtive Phil Fields*

Some remarkable actors who can make you laugh and then tear your heart out later on are Mickey Rooney, Jack Nicholson, Katherine Hepburn, Donald Pleasence, Tallulah Bankhead, and Vittorio Gassman. Jason Robards is in a class by himself.

"The world is a comedy to those that think and a tragedy to those that feel." — Horace Walpole

Federico Fellini, master of the nuance employed as comment, is also a skilled hand at low comedy. His vaudeville sequence in "Roma" is a work of art. Fellini's favorite American film, "Twentieth Century," which I've seen at least 40 times, feature the one and only John Barrymore and the matchless comedienne, Carol Lombard. Luis Bunuel's genius never flags. Jean Renoir is in a class by himself.

Roland Young, Myrna Loy, Nichols and May, Melvin Douglas, Roz Russell, William Powell, Ina Clair and Spencer Tracy never had to push for laughs. Neither did Noel-Noel, Mary Astor, and The Lunts. Peter Lorre was in a class by himself.

(About critics) "They got the map but they can't drive the bus." — Jackie Gleason

If I had to choose a play that made me laugh more than any other it would be "A Flea in Her Ear" by Feydeau as performed by The Comedie Francaise, with "Le Dindon" by the same author a close second. Every actor in that extraordinary company is a sight laugh to begin with and shows the audience no mercy right through the bows. I was an ecstatic victim.

The great entertainers, Jimmy Durante, Sammy Davis, Bea Lillie, George Burns, The Ritz Brothers; make you feel so good. When Jonathan Winters is rolling the way he did when improvising as the busdriver for the Tommy Dorsey band he is as funny as anyone. Redd Foxx and Jackie Miles are in the Comedy Hall of Fame. Milton Berle is the greatest standup comic.

"I noticed something long ago when I worked for The Marx Brothers. We would watch audiences emerge from the previews of their pictures helpless with laughter, tears streaking down their faces. A minute later their faces would freeze and they'd say "Wasn't that silly?" But they'd go to a Garbo picture or a 'serious' play, come out with tears in their eyes and feel ennobled. People feel comedy is somehow beneath their dignity. They feel humor is trivial."— S.J. Perelman

Some memorable comic performances: Donald Sinden in "London Assurance," Clive Revill in "Oliver," Alec Guiness in "The Horse's Mouth," Alberto Sordi in "The White Sheik," Charpin in "Fanny" (French), Ruth Draper in "An Evening with Ruth Draper," Rex Harrison and Stanley Holloway in "My Fair Lady" (Broadway Production), Judy Holliday in "Born Yesterday" (Broadway Production).

97

Television: There isn't any need for dubbed laughter or
a sweetened sound track in "Rumpole of the Bailey."
Leo McKern and the cast are perfection. Bob Hoskins and
Frances de la Tour scintillate in "Flickers." Robert Morley
and Peter Ustinov make any talk show worthwhile. Buddy
Hackett can break it up pretty good and Jonathan Miller is
probably the most engaging raconteur since GBS. Johnny
Carson deals with comedy beautifully and is absolutely
fearless when it comes to way out humor. Bless him. I
always take my phone off the hook to watch Benny Hill,
Phil Silvers, Rodney Dangerfield, Gleason and Carney,
John Cleese, "Barney Miller" and "Odd Couple " reruns,
Burnett and Korman, Ronnie Barker and Leonard Rossiter.

Tyrone Guthrie. A true Homme De Theatre who was at
home with Pirandello and Wilde, as he was with Shakespeare
and Wilder. Anyone interested in theater should read his
book "A Life in the Theater." Anyone serious about comedy
should reread Joyce Cary's trilogy on the artist Gully
Jimson and Sean O'Casey's plays. And while you're at it
take another look at "June Moon," "Three Men on a Horse,"
"Once in a Lifetime," "Room Service," and "The Odd
Couple," all American classics, Fred Allen was unique.
A.J. Liebling, Robert Benchley, S.J. Perelman, and George
S. Kaufman were major along with their grandpa, Mark Twain.

Why does every pedant trying to come on as a hipster
employ the euphemism "schtick" to try and convince
those in the know that he knows? The comic genius, Raimu,
was the Emperor of schtick, French schtick to be sure, but
schtick nevertheless. Tricks the actor uses to evoke
laughter. Acting is full of tricks. The best actors do not

allow the audience to see them. When they can see you acting you are dead. Garson Kanin says writing a play is in a way a trick.

I've always laughed at Ted Healy, Ian Carmichael, Jack Weston, Guy Marks, Edward Brophy, Red Buttons, Teddy Hart, Lou Jacobi, Charlotte Rae, Dudley Moore, Franklin Pangborn, Irene Handl, William Frawley, Louis Nye, Toto, Sheila Hancock, Hugh Herbert, Stiller and Meara, and Terry-Thomas.

Samuel Beckett had Laurel and Hardy in mind when he wrote "Waiting for Godot." Bert Lahr starred in the play on Broadway. He was unforgettable. I wrote him a note telling him Raimu would have been jealous and he phoned and said "I don't know what the hell it's all about but I love doing it."

"A comedian is closer to humanity than a tragedian. He learns not to take himself too seriously. A tragedian, thinking always of his noble part, becomes in the end somewhat ignoble. Comedians are much more valuable to the theater than tragedians. They can do both and their tragedy when they tackle it has a warmth the tragedian never knows." — Laurence Olivier

the Author:
Eddie Lawrence ...

first appeared in New York at the Radio City Music Hall
where he did his act, a wild conglomeration of non-sequiters
including an impersonation of Ronald Colman being held
up in Greenwich Village, Charles Boyer broadcasting the
Louis-Schmeling fight, and a weepy, Jolson-like character
known as Sentimental Max who later developed into the
now famous "Old Philosopher." Afterwards, he was engaged
by the Roxy, only a block away, to write and direct
comedy sketches between film screenings.

War broke out and Eddie went into the medical corps.
While serving in a field hospital in North Africa he was
spotted by Major Andre Baruch during his appendectomy.
He'd remembered Eddie from a variety show in New York
and got him transferred to the American Expeditionary
Stations where Lawrence wrote and directed a series of
live shows for American and British troops featuring Ella
Logan, Humphrey Bogart, Annabella, John Marley, Bruce
Cabot, Leo Durocher and Field Marshall Alexander.

Back in the U.S. he teamed up with Marley in the popular
radio show "Lawrence and Marley," a forerunner of "Laugh-
In," "The Carol Burnett Show," and even "Monte Python."
They were wild. Eddie introduced "The Old Philosopher"
character on the Steve Allen Sunday Show and NBC
surrounded him with a staff of eight, including Woody
Allen, marking him for "development."

After hanging around for months, Lawrence escaped to
Paris and remained there for five years. He wrote the
French film, "The Ladies and the Men," and three one-
act plays. They were produced at the Provincetown Play-

house while he stayed on in Paris, and received enthusiastic notices. He also studied painting, his first profession, with the French master Fernand Leger and appeared in several motion pictures.

He returned to America to write a series of comedy shorts for Paramount, and Victor Borge's television show. He also wrote for Bert Lahr, Jack E. Leonard, and Sid Caesar.

Eddie recorded nine record albums and is featured along with Nichols and May, Mel Brooks and Lennie Bruce on Warner's "Twenty-Five Years of Comedy." He's appeared on the Johnny Carson Show forty times. On Broadway he created the role of Sandor the Bookie in "Bells are Ringing" starring Judy Holliday, and played Banjo in "Sherry," the musical version of "The Man Who Came To Dinner." He also appeared in "The Threepenny Opera" during the legendary seven year run at the De Lys Theater.

Among his film roles are Scratch Wallace in "The Night They Raided Minsky's", Eric Von Stroheim in "The Wild Party", and assorted wisecracking GI's in French films.

Mr. Lawrence wrote the original Book and Lyrics for "Kelly," the controversial musical of the sixties. He likes to stress the word "original" because of the merciless, unauthorized reworking of the show during the out-of-town tryout. It pleases him no end that the record album of of the original Kelly score as sung by the composer, Moose Charlap, and Eddie, and recorded for the most part in Charlap's den, now graces the windows of the major record shops.

Mr. Lawrence is married to the Australian Designer, Marilyn Bligh-White. They have a son, Garrett.

Lawrence's musical based on the life of Paul Gaugin, "The Expressionist," with music by Mr. Charlap, has been optioned. His plays, "Louis and the Elephant," "Sort of an Adventure," and "The Beautiful Mariposa" have been produced on and off Broadway.

"The Natives were Restless" is a play about Paris and some of the ex-GI's who stayed on. "A Nose for a Nose" is Mr. Lawrence's latest play. It's a farce — very contemporary.

Lawrence did a nightly newscast from a hut near Caserta, Italy in 1945. It was the only news in English that came in loud and clear in Yalta. One night, Mr. Churchill lit up his after-dinner cigar and beckoned to Mr. Roosevelt, mumbling, "Well, let's see what Sergeant Lawrence has to say to us tonight." There were witnesses.